MAKING CITIZE

Can social studies classrooms be effective "makers" of citizens if much of what occurs in these classrooms does little to prepare young people to participate in the civic and political life of our democracy? *Making Citizens* illustrates how social studies can recapture its civic purpose through an approach that incorporates meaningful civic learning into middle and high school classrooms. The book explains why social studies teachers, particularly those working in diverse and urban areas, should infuse civic education into their teaching, and outlines how this can be done effectively.

Directed at both pre-service and in-service social studies teachers and designed for easy integration into social studies methods courses, this book follows students and teachers in social studies classrooms as they experience a new approach to the traditional, history-oriented social studies curriculum that uses themes, essential questions, discussion, writing, current events, and action research to explore enduring civic questions. Following the experiences of three teachers working at three diverse high schools, Beth C. Rubin considers how social studies classrooms might become places where young people study, ponder, discuss, and write about relevant civic questions while they learn history. She draws upon the latest sociocultural theories on youth civic identity development to describe a field-tested approach to civic education that takes into consideration the classroom and curricular constraints faced by new teachers.

Beth C. Rubin is Associate Professor in the Department of Educational Theory, Policy, and Administration at Rutgers University where she is co-coordinator of the social studies education program.

MAKING CITIZENS

Transforming Civic Learning for
Diverse Social Studies Classrooms

Beth C. Rubin

Routledge
Taylor & Francis Group

NEW YORK AND LONDON

First published 2012
by Routledge
711 Third Avenue, New York, NY 10017

Simultaneously published in the UK
by Routledge
2 Park Square, Milton Park, Abingdon, Oxon OX14 4RN

Routledge is an imprint of the Taylor & Francis Group, an informa business

Library of Congress Cataloging-in-Publication Data
Rubin, Beth C.
  Making citizens : transforming civic learning for diverse social studies classrooms / Beth C. Rubin.
     p. cm.
  1. Citizenship—Study and teaching—United States. 2. Civics—Study and teaching—United States. 3. Social sciences—Study and teaching—United States. 4. Cultural pluralism—United States. 5. Education—Social aspects—United States. I. Title.
  LC1091.R83 2011
  372.83'2—dc22   2011000557

ISBN: 978–0–415–87461–8 (hbk)
ISBN: 978–0–415–87462–5 (pbk)
ISBN: 978–0–203–81308–9 (ebk)

Typeset in Bembo
by Keystroke, Station Road, Codsall, Wolverhampton

"I cannot teach anybody anything, I can only make them think."
—Socrates

This book is dedicated to Lois Rubin, John Sutula,
Ed Abbott, Theodore Sizer, and Anne Haas Dyson,
five outstanding educators whose respect for the curiosity,
humanity, and intelligence of their students will forever
influence my path as a teacher.

CONTENTS

Acknowledgements   ix

1   Introduction: Transforming Social Studies Education
    Through Meaningful Civic Learning   1

2   Essentially Different: Using Essential Questions and
    Themes for Civic Learning   21

3   Talking Civics: Open Discussion in the Social Studies
    Classroom   41

4   Civic Communications: Writing and Expression for Civic
    Learning   67

5   Beyond "Current Events Fridays": Connecting Past to
    Present All Year Long   97

6   What's the Problem? Civic Action Research in the Social
    Studies Classroom   117

References   *141*
About the Author   *147*
Index   *149*

ACKNOWLEDGEMENTS

I am forever indebted to the three teachers featured in this book (because of confidentiality rules they cannot be named) who so bravely and creatively co-developed and implemented the curriculum and teaching practices described in these pages. They welcomed me and my research assistants into their classrooms and shared their reflections openly. The process made their teaching far more public than is usually the case, and they bore this friendly scrutiny with grace and good humor. Their dedication to the goals of the project and their willingness to reconstruct their entire U.S. History II curricula was impressive and critical to the project's success.

I am always impressed and inspired by high school and middle school students, and those participating in this project were no exception. The students in the three study schools jumped wholeheartedly into ways of doing social studies that were unfamiliar to most of them. The students were frank and insightful in our individual conversations with them, and they were cheerfully tolerant of our presence in their classrooms.

A wonderful group of assistants joined me during the design and research phases of this project. Brian Hayes, graduate student researcher extraordinaire, brought a wealth of social studies and classroom expertise to his work on the project, greatly enriching our curriculum development, implementation, and research process. Undergraduate research assistants Brian Canares, Kate Maley, Enrique Noguera, and Jennifer Turley visited classrooms and interviewed students with enthusiasm and care.

I was supported by many in the writing of this book. Carl and Britt Wish allowed me to use their apartment as a writers' retreat, making Chapters 1 and 2 possible. Sara Elinoff Acker retreated with me for three days on a writing-eating-yoga binge at Kripalu in Western Massachusetts, during which time I finished Chapter 3 and got Chapter 4 into shape. Chapter 5 was crafted across a library table from Thea Abu El-Haj, inspiring each other's powers of concentration. Ben Justice valiantly read and commented on the entire manuscript, an act of true collegial solidarity. Heather Dunham, an outstanding new teacher and recent GSE graduate, provided essential proofreading and feedback at a point when I had completely run out of steam. Catherine Bernard, my wonderful editor at Routledge, shared insightful comments that greatly improved the manuscript.

My ideas about teaching and research in the service of personal and social betterment have been influenced by many people. I am especially grateful for what I have learned from Pedro Noguera, Judith Warren Little, Ilana Horn, Tom Stritikus, Amanda Godley, Lance McCready, Jean Yonemura Wing, Susan Yonezawa, Makeba Jones, Bradley Levinson, Ben Kirshner, Michelle Fine, Thea Abu El-Haj, Jim Giarelli, Terrie Epstein, Mayida Zaal, Jennifer Ayala, Diana Hess, Walter Parker, Patricia Avery, Joe Kahne, Joel Westheimer, and Meira Levinson.

This research would not have been possible without the financial support I received from the Spencer Foundation, the Rutgers Research Council, and the Rutgers Graduate School of Education. For non-financial support, my parents and brother, Lois, Ira, and Joel Rubin, provided a home experience that nurtured discussion, critical thinking, and engagement with the world. Today my children, Maya and Kai, and my husband Dave Wish provide haven and inspiration. My children have given me first hand insight into the worlds of young people in school; they serve as daily reminders of the trust and hope that children put in the adults who are responsible for them at school. My husband is an object lesson in selfless dedication to creating learning experiences that touch people's whole selves. More important than all of that, however, are the endless laughter and cozy snuggles that I am blessed to be part of each day.

1

INTRODUCTION

Transforming Social Studies Education Through Meaningful Civic Learning

Making Citizens

In the spring of 2010 the Texas State Board of Education made and sustained headlines as they debated and ultimately legislated the content of the state's U.S. History curriculum. Concerned about the "left-wing tilt"[1] of the U.S. History curriculum, the board

> approved a social studies curriculum that will put a conservative stamp on history and economics textbooks, stressing the superiority of American capitalism, questioning the Founding Fathers' commitment to a purely secular government and presenting Republican political philosophies in a more positive light.
>
> *(McKinley Jr., 2010)*

Later that same spring, state legislators in Arizona decided that another area of the social studies curriculum, ethnic studies, was inappropriate for the state's high school students. State schools Superintendent Tom Horne, speaking on May 12, 2010, explained that ethnic studies "is conveying a revolutionary message, a separatist message, a message that makes students hostile toward the United States, which is a country that they will be citizens of, they will be living in"(*Arizona Daily Star*, 2010). In May, Governor Jan Brewer signed a law aimed to end ethnic studies in Arizona schools (*New York Times*, 2010).

---

1 In March 2010 Texas State Board of Education member Don McLeroy explained, "What we have is the history profession, the experts, seem to have a left-wing tilt, so what we were doing is trying to restore some balance to the standards" (Grinberg, 2010).

Challenges to social studies curricula do not only come from the conservative side of the political spectrum. In 1990 the Oakland, California school board, under pressure from citizen groups including the National Association for the Advancement of Colored People, Chinese for Affirmative Action, the National Chicano Moratorium Committee, the Bay Area affiliate of the National Coalition of Education Activists, among many others, voted against adopting the state approved Houghton Mifflin History–Social Science series for kindergarten through eighth grade. A citizen group, Communities United Against Racism in Education (CURE), lobbied hard against the books. As sociologist Todd Gitlin wrote:

> CURE pointed to some genuine instances of establishment bias . . . But CURE and other critics did themselves no favors by interspersing valid criticisms among scores of indiscriminate ones. They were so eager to find ethnocentrism in these texts that they seemed to quarrel with the notion that there was or is a dominant American culture . . . When the books singled out minorities' customs, CURE saw disapproval; when the books didn't single them out, they saw neglect.
>
> *(1996, pp. 9–10)*

Debates over the content of the social studies curriculum were and continue to be of great interest to a range of people both within the states within which such controversies take place and nationally. Parents, lawmakers, historians, teachers, politicians, activists, advocacy groups, students, and others weigh in, often passionately, on these discussions of what ought to be taught to public school students in their social studies classrooms, with all parties expressing deep concern about the content of U.S. students' social studies instruction and the impact of this content on the beliefs and proclivities of our future citizens.

What draws my attention in these cases is not so much the content of the debates or the predictably polarized politics they mark. Rather I would like to highlight something else reflected in these struggles over curricula—the common notion, held by people from all segments of the ideological spectrum, that the social studies curriculum has implications for students' sense of themselves as citizens; the idea, unquestioned by right or left, that what is taught in our social studies classrooms matters profoundly and has the potential to shape students' civic identities in particular ways. This belief in the citizen-making power of the social studies has fueled curriculum battles for decades.[2]

---

2 In the 1940s, for example, Harold Rugg's popular 14-volume social studies textbook series, published under the general title *Man and His Changing Society,* was attacked for espousing socialist values. In a more recent example, in 1994 the United States Senate voted 99–1 to reject the National History Standards developed by the National Center for History in the Schools. Standards critic Lynne Cheney explained, "We are a better people than the National Standards indicate, and our children deserve to know it" (Cheney, 1994).

With this in mind, one might expect that social studies classrooms might be seething cauldrons of conflict and debate on pressing national concerns, as some might argue would befit incubators of citizenship. Or perhaps we might predict that they would be inspiring hothouses of patriotism and civic spirit, as others might desire. Yet, as most of us might recall from hours spent in K-12 social studies classrooms, neither of these are accurate descriptions of the school social studies experience in the United States. "All we did was watch movies, handouts, dittos," remarked Juan, student at an urban high school. "Teachers just give you the book, read out of it, do the work, that's it," reflected Sarah, student at a middle class suburban school. "The teachers' don't teach . . . they'll give us a worksheet and we'll have to read it and then just answer the questions," Sean, student at a different suburban school, concurred. These comments, a few of many similar sentiments expressed by public high school students talking about their previous year's social studies classes, hint at how classroom social studies is frequently experienced in the United States.

Over and over in my research and in the research of others, students describe their experiences in social studies classrooms as distinctly unmemorable. Danny, an 11th grade student at Allwood High, a diverse, middle class suburban high school, reflected upon the previous year in U.S. history, saying,

> I forgot all the stuff we did last year. Except for a couple minor details . . .
> I'm not interested in the whole, you know, George Washington thing.
> Because I feel like you go over that so often. It's just like, I'm sick of it. So
> I don't really pay attention.

Bennie, a student at an urban high school serving a low-income community, tells a similar tale. In his U.S. history class, he explains, "we talked about things that happened like 13,000 years ago, that don't got nothing to do with today." Neither instilling patriotism nor fostering civic questioning, it is difficult to make a case that social studies classrooms are vibrant centers of civic learning in the public school system. Indeed, much of what occurs in these classrooms has no direct relation to this charge, often frustrates both teachers and students, and may even contribute to students' sense of alienation from civic life (Knight Abowitz & Harnish, 2006). If this is where citizens are "made," what kinds of citizens do such practices make?

Students in most social studies classrooms study history chronologically, learn passively, and encounter the story of the United States as one that is already written, in which citizens are witnesses to history rather than active participants in the narrative. Teachers in these settings feel rushed to "cover" as much as possible, fear "leaving something out," and are continually frustrated by never being able to "get to today" in their instruction.

Such instructional choices have consequences for students' civic learning. Learning, in general, takes place amid social settings and interactions. Rather than a process taking place solely within an individual's brain, people are social animals whose learning is shaped by who is there, what is being done, what materials and activities are available, and what interactions are taking place (Greeno & MMAP, 1998; Lave, 1993; Lave & Wenger, 1991). For example, students in a social studies classroom in which the most frequent educational activities are listening to lectures, reading the textbook, and completing close-ended worksheets and question sets may come to understand social studies as a set of information to be heard, memorized, and reproduced for assessment purposes. On the other hand, students learning in a social studies classroom in which reading, discussion, and writing about controversial and relevant topics is commonplace may understand social studies to be a grappling with relevant and contested issues about which they must form and re-form opinions. This is called a "situated" understanding of learning, and its implications for civic learning and identity are significant. If we wish to cultivate an active, engaged citizenry, then social studies teaching curricula and practices must be designed to reflect and achieve this aim.

This book aims to provide an example of social studies curricula and teaching practices in general, and for U.S. history in particular, that run counter to those described above. Built on current understandings of how diverse young people come to see themselves as citizens, the project described in this book aimed to "make" engaged, critical and skilled citizens able to think deeply about ongoing civic issues and see themselves as participants in our nation's civic discourse. This book is designed specifically for social studies educators who are looking for compelling examples of how to recover the civic learning aims of social studies, and practical suggestions for how to structure their classrooms to better "make" the engaged citizens we hope our social studies instruction will create.

Diverse Young People and Civic Learning

What sorts of social studies practices might provide for meaningful civic learning? Let us look at an episode of engaged civic inquiry for insight. In this snippet from classroom life in an urban middle school social studies classroom, students engaged in a lively discussion of the Pledge of Allegiance. Amber, Jessica, and Angelica wrestle here with notions of justice, individual rights, and allegiance.

Amber: WE [loudly] are the one nation, under God—one nation.
Jessica: When the Pledge of Allegiance says "under God," it can't actually say that and expect people to pledge allegiance to the flag, because there's other races that really don't BELIEVE in God. So if you don't believe in God, why would you pledge allegiance to the flag that states, "Under God?" You won't . . . it's
. . .
Angelica: Well, me and her [referring to another student] were discussing. She said that it's not one nation because of segre. . . . like we had segregation, all this stuff, all this hate. But you're not pledging to the people IN America, you're pledging TO AMERICA itself.

This brief slice of classroom conversation displays students' potential for interest in and engagement with complex civic questions. Who is the "one nation" invoked in the Pledge? Does our nation's history of segregation and "all this hate" provide a challenge to this notion? Can all Americans be expected to agree to a pledge that invokes belief in a deity? What about those "other races" who don't believe in God; can they be expected to make the same pledge?

Although quantitative measures of civic attainment consistently rank low-income African American and Latino students behind their White and more affluent peers, Amber, Jessica, Angelica, and their classmates—African American and Latino eighth-grade students at a middle school in a low-income urban area—energetically pursued such questions for over two hours, leaving the room reluctantly and still talking. Their personal and community experiences sparked their interest in the discussion, the discussion format encouraged their interaction with each other and with the text, and their engagement with ongoing civic issues was authentic and heartfelt.

Curricular and instructional practices that encourage the interplay between students' daily lives and larger civic issues provide opportunities for this sort of meaningful civic learning. Decades of quantitative study of youth civic knowledge and beliefs give us a lot of information about what students do and do not know as measured by adult-determined measures of significant civic knowledge. Such studies, however, give us little insight into what is actually meaningful and relevant to students as they enter into civic learning. Yet these are the tools and materials that students use to make sense of the social studies curriculum, as we see in the example above. A better sense of how civic identity is shaped can inform curriculum planning in powerful ways.

As youth move amid distinct community and school contexts they have a variety of experiences that shape them as citizens, some positive, some more complicated. Students' daily experiences inform how they make sense of what they learn in the social studies curriculum. Do students experience "liberty and justice" in their daily lives? Do they have reason to believe that their rights, as expressed in the Bill of Rights, will be upheld, or have they seen or experienced violations of these rights? Students who see civic ideals mesh with civic realities in their daily lives experience "congruence" between ideals and realities, while those who see a conflict experience "disjuncture."

Students also have a variety of perspectives on civic action. Some feel that to be a good citizen one need only to pay one's taxes, obey the law, and vote. Other students believe that good citizenship involves taking action to remedy civic problems. Students who see good citizenship as a matter of not doing wrong take a more "passive" approach, while those who think it calls for action hold a more "active" stance.

When we consider these two aspects of civic identity development in tandem, we can picture youth civic identity existing on a range. Table 1.1, developed from a study of middle and high school students' perspectives on and

TABLE 1.1 Typology of Civic Identity

		Students' experiences in relation to the learned ideals of the United States	
		CONGRUENCE	*DISJUNCTURE*
Students' attitudes toward civic participation	ACTIVE	Quadrant I: **Aware** *Change is needed for equity and fairness*	Quadrant II: **Empowered** *Change is a personal and community necessity*
	PASSIVE	Quadrant III: **Complacent** *No change is necessary, all is well in the U.S.*	Quadrant IV: **Discouraged** *No change is possible, life in the U.S. is unfair.*

A version of this table first appeared in Rubin (2007).

experiences with civic life (Rubin, 2007), graphically represents this range of civic identity.

Aware students are those who have not personally experienced a clash between what they learn are the precepts of the United States and what they have experienced, but they are aware that such clashes exist and they express a desire to work for change. As one such student commented, "I am not like 'down with the government' or anything. But I know that I am more aware of some social injustices . . . I know that since I am a citizen I can do something about it."

In the previous study, these students attributed their awareness to school-based discussions and activities, such as in-class discussions about inequality and curricular units on social justice movements, as well as family influences.

Similar to the aware students, *complacent* students experience a mesh between the ideals and realities of life in the United States; they personally have experienced safety and opportunity. Unlike their aware peers, however, these students express a rather passive attitude toward civic participation. One such student, for example, described a good citizen as a person who lived his or her life "to the fullest in the nation, abiding by laws . . . just enjoying being in the place, not worrying completely about politics or what's concerning the world outside."

Complacent students generalize from their own experiences to conclude that life in the United States is generally fair for everyone; as they feel satisfied with the status quo, they tend not to see a need to work for change and may criticize those who do for "making a big deal out of nothing." In contrast to aware students, complacent students tend not to come into contact with peers whose life circumstances differ from their own, and their social studies classes have done little to challenge their beliefs that the system is working well for everyone.

Discouraged students are those who experience a gap between civic ideals and the realities of their daily lives and are not optimistic about using civic action to address these gaps. These students have experienced discrimination, rights violations, violence in their communities, and connections to historical injustices. For these students, often from low-income, urban schools, such experiences are powerful daily reminders of the persistent inequalities of U.S. society that they feel cannot be assuaged through civic action. As one student explained:

> I feel I could do things, but I don't feel it would make a difference because people are down on children, like we can't really do anything . . . He [Martin Luther King] did a right thing, but other people who were against it did wrong, and I think it's going to happen all over again.

Some students in the earlier study moved back and forth between discouraged and empowered identities, revealing mixed feelings about whether or not change was possible. However, certain classroom practices, as well as family and community role models, seemed to nudge students toward the more hopeful and engaged orientation as described below.

Like their discouraged peers, *empowered* students have directly experienced the gap between civic ideals and realities. Yet these students remain passionate about the need to be civically active and work for change. As one student commented, "If I find an opportunity for me to get my rights, I'm going to try and take it!"

Similar to aware students, empowered students describe their social studies classes as pivotal to their understanding of their own rights and avenues for action. One such student recounted learning about "freedom of speech, freedom of petition, freedom of the press, and [the illegality of] search and seizure" in her social studies class. Before that, she said, "I had no idea about the amendments . . . and about our rights that we do have and don't have." This change-oriented identity seems to be connected to such social studies practices as simulations, discussions, and writing activities designed to connect course content to their lives and concerns. Within this framework, a primary purpose of civic education is to help students move from *complacent* to *aware*, from *discouraged* to *empowered*.

Across school settings, in the previous study, students in social studies classrooms in which they were encouraged to identify and explore civic problems appeared to develop more actively engaged civic identities. Yet most social studies classes are not structured to take into account or build upon students' varying experiences with civic life; many educators choose to avoid controversial social and civic issues in their classrooms, and discussions like the Pledge of Allegiance seminar depicted earlier are rare. Moreover, recent research points to a significant gap between the civic learning opportunities available to students in low-income communities and those available to their peers in higher-income communities (Kahne & Middaugh, 2008; Levinson, 2007). Kahne and Middaugh, in their study of a nationally representative sample of ninth graders, found that low-income students, students not heading to college, and students of color had less access to best practices in civic education, such as open discussion of civic issues and issues of personal importance, service learning, and study of community problems.

If students' civic orientations are shaped through their daily experiences within particular schools and communities and influenced by factors well beyond civics lessons and textbooks, then we are faced with a challenge if we continue to avoid engaging directly with students' experiences yet desire to encourage active citizenship. Engaging students in active consideration of the civic problems they encounter in their daily lives and incorporating them into ongoing civic discourse holds potential for fostering more aware and empowered civic identities in all youth (Fine et al., 2007; Kahne & Westheimer, 2003; Parker & Hess, 2001; Rubin, 2007).

Indeed, instructional practices that engage youth in considering problematic aspects of U.S. civic society can benefit *all* students. Frank discussion of civic rights, processes, and social disparities can encourage a more active civic identity, empowering youth who have experienced a gap between civic ideals and realities and challenging students who have not experienced this gap to look beyond their immediate concerns. While such a "problem-posing" approach is nothing new (see Freire, 1970), its application to classroom-based social studies education represents a departure from traditional models of civic education and research.

Crafting a New Approach

This book describes one approach to integrating meaningful civic learning into middle and high school social studies classrooms. It uses the experiences of teachers and students trying out this new approach in three public high schools to illustrate how social studies might recapture its civic purpose and how social studies classrooms can become places where young people study, ponder, discuss, write about, and grapple with large civic questions while they are learning history.

This book is premised unambiguously on the conviction that it is beneficial to individuals and to our society as a whole for young people to become engaged, empowered, thinking citizens. As author, I am inspired and gratified by how Vincent, a student at one of the participating high schools, tied our teaching methods and curricular approaches together with a statement of belief in the power of citizens to shape civic life. He reflected,

> one of the essential questions whenever we took a test was . . . "Who has the ability to make a change?" And I think, you know, people. The general public has an ability, you know, they have the ability to make a chance. We as the public, we can change things. We have the power to change.

In this book we get to know three teachers and their students, working and living in diverse communities, as they engage in a new approach, based upon new understandings of youth civic identity development, to the history-oriented social studies curriculum. *Making Citizens: Transforming Civic Learning for Diverse Social Studies Classrooms* shows social studies teachers why and how their classrooms can be transformed into powerful sites for civic learning, places where students and teachers can come to believe that "we have the power to change."

New understandings of youth civic identity development indicate that traditional social studies curricula and pedagogies need to be radically transformed if we are serious about creating civic learning opportunities for all students. Currently there are many specialized courses, mini-units, and discrete activities developed by civic education advocates that have been implemented in schools and classrooms, but these efforts are not widespread and generally do not integrate the lived experiences of traditionally underserved students into mandated courses.

If the goal is to transform the civic learning experiences of all students, state mandated social studies courses, particularly U.S. history, which is universally required of high school students in the United States, are the most widely available sites where students might experience meaningful civic learning. This project, then, began with an essential question of its own: how might the required U.S. History II class be turned into an opportunity for meaningful civic learning while still teaching the required content? What would a U.S. History II course look like if it was built upon the notion that students' civic identities are shaped by their daily lives and experiences amid the contexts of classroom practices and community life?

Drawing upon the theoretical framework and research findings outlined earlier in this chapter, the instructional reform project described in this book used four design principles, shown in Box 1.1, to frame the development of social studies teaching practices to take into account, indeed capitalize upon, students' daily experiences, social positions, and passion for such issues.

BOX 1.1 DESIGN PRINCIPLES FOR MEANINGFUL CIVIC LEARNING IN DIVERSE SETTINGS

1. Civic education should build upon students' own experiences with civic life, including daily experiences with civic institutions (e.g. schools, police).
2. Civic education should provide opportunities for students to consider and discuss key issues and controversies in civic life.
3. Civic education should build students' discussion, analysis, critique, and research skills.
4. Civic education should build students' knowledge of their rights and responsibilities as citizens in a way that connects directly to their own concerns.

To accomplish this goal, the project team employed a design-based research (DBR) approach to develop, apply, and investigate a new approach to civic education in the high school social studies curriculum. DBR involves "'engineering' particular forms of learning and systematically studying those forms of learning within the context" as a "means of addressing the complexity that is a hallmark of educational settings" (Cobb et al., 2003, p. 9). Such projects are both "generative and transformative," creating new forms of learning based on specific ideas about practices, studying those innovations, and using analysis of this process to refine the practices under study, gain insight, and produce models of successful innovation (Kelly, 2003, p.3). Frequently employed in studies of mathematical and scientific learning, DBR has rarely been used in social studies research. The nature of this study, however, made it a highly useful methodology as the research team designed, implemented, and tracked the implementation of a new approach to social studies education based upon a theoretically and empirically derived set of design principles.

In the first stage of the study, the study team—myself (a university professor), a Ph.D. student, three teachers, and three undergraduate interns—met intensively to discuss the design principles described in Table 1.2 and develop curricular and pedagogical approaches that integrated the principles into the required curriculum for the upcoming school year. We began by reorganizing the teachers' U.S. History II curricula into thematic segments undergirded by essential questions, the process and results of which will be described in detail in Chapter 2. The team then drew from the literature on best practices in civic education and meaningful

TABLE 1.2 Civic Skill Building Strands

	Discussion	*Writing and expression*	*Current events*	*Civic action research*
Strand	Seminar Take-a-Stand Structured conversation	Social studies journals Persuasive letter Persuasive speech Newscast Five paragraph essay	As related to themes Connected to questions Connected to election	Problem identification Research solutions Presentation
Purpose	Develop discussion and listening skills, ability to analyze and present a well-supported opinion on a controversial issue.	Develop skills of written and oral expression, ability to work alone or in a group to prepare/present.	To weave students' consideration of current events into themes, events, and questions under study.	Develop ability to investigate public issues and concerns using primary and secondary sources, to develop a plan for action.

social studies instruction to develop four "strands" designed to thread civic learning throughout the academic year. These strands are briefly outlined below in Table 1.2, and will be described in detail in Chapters 3–6.

During the second stage of the study, the teachers implemented the approach in their U.S. History II classes. The research team observed frequently in each class, and the entire project team met monthly to continue discussion and curriculum development. The principal investigator interviewed the teachers at the beginning and end of the school year. Students were surveyed and interviewed to learn about their experiences with the curriculum, and student work was collected throughout the year. For this book, findings are reported in five separate chapters focusing on themes and questions, discussion, writing and expression, civic action research, and current events, although there was overlap among these categories.

Allwood, Oak Knoll, and Surrey—Three Diverse American Communities

The communities within which each of the study schools were located provide a good example of the many forms that diversity can take in the United States. Allwood, Surrey, and Oak Knoll, all within 65 miles of each other, had distinct profiles and concerns, providing rich contexts for implementation of a curriculum premised on the idea that for civic learning to be meaningful it should be open to students' lives and experiences.

Located in a densely populated area on the eastern seaboard of the United States, *Allwood*, a town of roughly 100,000, experienced rapid growth in the past 10 years. Allwood High School, one of two comprehensive high schools in Allwood, was located in the southern region of the town and served a less affluent slice of the Allwood population than the town's second high school in the north. The Allwood population was 46.6% White, 35.1% Asian American (with 18% of Allwood students reporting Asian Indian ancestry), 8.5% African American and 8.4% Latino. Adults in the community worked in education and healthcare, professional and technical fields, finance and insurance, hospitality industries, retail, manufacturing, and construction.

The median household income of Allwood families in 2007 was $80,581, although the families of Allwood High School students were about $20,000 below that and 15.5% of Allwood High School students were eligible for free or reduced lunch. Unemployment in Allwood, as of 2007, was 4.2%, with a 6.4% poverty rate for individuals and a 2.7% rate for families. Among the three communities in our study, Allwood was the safest. Its violent crime rate of 1.67 fell well below the state and national averages; a person's chances of being a victim of a violent crime such as murder, rape, armed robbery, or assault in Allwood was 1 in 600, compared to 1 in 282 at the state level. Allwood's property crime rate was also low at 17.2 per 1000 residents. The number of crimes occurring annually per square mile in Allwood was 60, on a par with the state.

Oak Knoll was a suburban community of roughly 44,000 located on the fringe of several heavily populated cities in the same northeastern state. A diverse town, Oak Knoll's residents were 53.9% White, 21.6% African American, 15.2% Latino, 7.6% Asian, and 1.3% other. Many White Oak Knoll families sent their children to private religious schools, thus the demographics of Oak Knoll High School did not mirror those of the community. Adults in the community were employed in a range of settings, predominantly professional, technical, and education and healthcare related, as well as retail, construction, transportation, arts, and public administration.

The unemployment rate in Oak Knoll, as of 2007, was 5.9%, the poverty rate for individuals was 5.2% and for families with children under 18 was 6.9%. The crime rate in Oak Knoll fell well below the state and national averages, with a violent crime rate of 2.1 per 1000 residents and a property crime rate of 22.96 per 1000 residents. The median household income in Oak Knoll was $90,000, which far surpasses both state and national numbers, yet 27% of the student population at Oak Knoll High School qualify for free or reduced lunch, reflecting the difference in town and school population characteristics.

Surrey was a small and densely populated declining post-industrial city of 80,000. In the 2000 census, the city's population was 53% African American, 38.8% Hispanic/Latino, 16.8% White, and 2.5% Asian. Far more people rented their homes in Surrey than owned them and median household income in Surrey, at $23,154, was well below the state average. Adults in Surrey worked in education and healthcare related jobs, food services and other service industries, and retail, construction, manufacturing, and professional sectors.

The unemployment rate in Surrey, as of 2007, was 16.1%, with 40.5% of individual Surrey residents living in poverty and 48.7% of families with children under the age of 18 subsisting below the poverty line. Frequently cited on lists of the most dangerous places to live in the United States, Surrey's violent crime rate of 22.8/1000 people meant the chance of being a victim of a violent crime (such as murder, rape, armed robbery, or assault) in Surrey was 1 in 44 compared to 1 out of 282 statewide. The rate of property crime in Surrey was even more dismal, with 1 out of 15 residents likely to be victims of burglary, theft, or motor vehicle theft. The population density of Surrey exacerbated the problem: whereas the national average for crimes per square mile is 49.6, in Surrey there were 699 crimes per square mile.

Students and Teachers in the Three Study Schools

The student demographics of Allwood, Oak Knoll, and Surrey were also a graphic representation of the many forms that "diversity" can take. Table 1.3 describes the demographics of the three participating schools in relation to race/ethnicity, socioeconomic status, language, and special education designation. While all three schools had significant numbers of students who spoke a language other than English at home and a large number of students with Individualized Education

TABLE 1.3 Student Demographics of Participating Schools

Allwood High School	Oak Knoll High School	Surrey High School
12% African American	42% African American	46% African American
27% Asian American	8% Asian American	2% Asian American
13% Latino	21.5% Latino	50% Latino
48% White	28% White	1% White
2.2% L.E.P.	4.9% L.E.P.	11.9% L.E.P.
42.4% speak language other than English at home	30.4% speak language other than English at home	43.3% speak language other than English at home
13.3% with I.E.P.s	15.4% with I.E.P.s	24.7% with I.E.P.s
4.9% mobility rate	7.7% mobility rate	29.5% mobility rate
14% free/reduced lunch	27% free/reduced lunch	65% free/reduced lunch

Plans (IEPs), Surrey's student mobility rate, the number of students meeting the federal income requirements for free and reduced lunch, and the number of Limited English Proficient (LEP) students far exceeded that of the other two schools.

Allwood and Oak Knoll both exceeded the state attendance rate of 94%, while Surrey fell far below the state average. Allwood's suspension rate of 36% far exceeded the state rate of 14%, indicating more stringent disciplinary policies, while Oak Knoll exceeded the state average by several percentage points, and Surrey dipped below, indicating a lack of disciplinary enforcement in the school that was reflected in the school hallways, full of students during class time, that the research team encountered during our visits. Table 1.4 displays disciplinary and attendance data for the three schools.

Even more striking were the differences in students' preparation for life after high school between the two suburban schools and the urban school in the study, as shown in Table 1.5. While Allwood and Oak Knoll students maintained high graduation rates, S.A.T. scores hovering just above or below the state averages, and a good percentage of juniors and seniors taking A.P. exams, Surrey High students dropped out of school at more than four times the rate of Allwood students and almost three times the rate of Oak Knoll students, had much lower graduation rates than students at the other two schools (with only 1 in 10 students passing the state test to graduate), they did poorly on the S.A.T., and A.P. participation was so minimal as to be negligible.

TABLE 1.4 Disciplinary and Attendance Data

Allwood High School	Oak Knoll High School	Surrey High School
Attendance: 96%	Attendance: 95%	Attendance: 80.1%
Suspensions: 36%	Suspensions: 21%	Suspensions: 10%
Expulsions: 0%	Expulsions: 0%	Expulsions: 0%

TABLE 1.5 Preparation for Life after High School

Allwood High School	Oak Knoll High School	Surrey High School
84% graduated by passing state test	78.2% graduated by passing state test	10.6% graduated by passing state test
256 took A.P. tests (15%)	490 took A.P. tests (26.6%)	29 took A.P. tests (4.3%)
S.A.T.: 533 math/500 verbal	S.A.T.: 493 math/474 verbal	S.A.T.: 330 math/335 verbal
Drop-out rate: 1.4%	Drop-out rate: 3%	Drop-out rate: 8.2%
Graduation rate: 97.4%	Graduation rate: 94.9%	Graduation rate: 75.3%
Post-graduation Plans: Four year college: 49.2% Two year college: 39.6% Other education: 2.5% Military: 1% Employment: 2.5% Undecided: 5.2%	Post-graduation Plans: Four year college: 69.9% Two year college: 27% Military: 0.5 % Employment: 1.8% Undecided: 0.7%	Post-graduation Plans: Four year college: 28% Two year college: 30.9% Other education: 17.4% Military: 1.9% Employment: 11.1% Undecided: 9.7% Other: 1%

Students at the three schools fared differently on state proficiency tests (see Table 1.6). Allwood High School students exceeded the state averages in both language arts literacy and mathematics. Oak Knoll students matched the state average in language arts literacy, but struggled in mathematics and fewer students reached advanced proficiency than the state average. Surrey High School students' scores, however, were consistently among the lowest in the state, with the majority of Surrey students not meeting proficiency levels. Indeed, according to the state department of education, the school was third from the bottom of all the public high schools in the state in terms of academic achievement.

TABLE 1.6 State Proficiency Testing Data for Allwood, Oak Knoll, Surrey, and State, 2006–7

		% not tested	Partial proficiency	Proficient	Advanced proficiency
State	Language Arts	0.8 %	13.5 %	66.3%	20.2%
	Mathematics	0.9%	25.1%	50.8%	24.2%
Allwood	Language Arts	0.5%	9.2%	71.4%	19.4%
	Mathematics	0.5%	21.1%	51.6%	27.3%
Oak Knoll	Language Arts	0.2%	13.6%	70.9%	15.5%
	Mathematics	0.6%	36.2%	46.2%	17.6%
Surrey	Language Arts	9.6%	62.4%	36.6%	1.1%
	Mathematics	8.7%	87.4%	9.5%	3.2%

In 2006–2007, all three schools failed to meet the annual yearly progress benchmarks set by the federal No Child Left Behind Act due to the performance of various subgroups on the statewide assessment. Table 1.7 describes this situation. While all three schools struggled to help their students with disabilities, students of color, and low-income students meet the proficiency threshold, Surrey's students' proficiency levels for students from these subgroups (groups that made up a major part of the Surrey student population) were dramatically lower than the other schools. In a school consisting almost entirely of low-income students of color, the small fraction of Surrey's African American, Latino, and economically disadvantaged students that met proficiency thresholds in mathematics and the close to two-thirds of these groups failing to meet the threshold in language arts literacy, raises the question of the viability of Surrey High School as an educational institution. While all three schools faced challenges meeting the needs of all of their students, as an educational institution Surrey High School was providing an experience for students very far below state and national expectations.

As with the schools as a whole, the student in the participating classrooms were a diverse group, and diverse in a variety of ways. Table 1.8 describes the student

TABLE 1.7 Subgroups Failing to Reach Proficiency Thresholds in 2006–7

	Language Arts Literacy *Proficiency threshold 79%*	**Mathematics** *Proficiency threshold 64%*
Allwood	64.5% of students with disabilities were proficient 78% of African American students were proficient	38.4% of students with disabilities were proficient 43.5% of African American students were proficient
Oak Knoll	50% of students with disabilities were proficient 70.2% of Hispanic students were proficient	20% of students with disabilities were proficient 55.2% of African American students were proficient 46% of Hispanic students were proficient 49.7% of economically disadvantaged students were proficient
Surrey	15% of students with disabilities were proficient 37.3% of African American students were proficient 43.4% of Hispanic students were proficient 39.3% of economically disadvantaged students were proficient	10.8% of African American students were proficient 15.1% of Hispanic students were proficient 9.5% of economically disadvantaged students were proficient

Table 1.8 Student Demographics and Tracks of Participating Classrooms

	Allwood High School	*Oak Knoll High School*	*Surrey High School*
Total number students	65	34	22
Classes/ tracks	3 classes 2nd highest level in a 4 tiered system	2 classes Lowest level in a 3 tiered system	2 classes Special education
Gender	26 male 39 female	19 male 15 female	18 male 4 female
Race/ ethnicity	6 African American 15 Asian American 5 Indian (South Asian) 8 Latino 4 Middle Eastern 29 White	19 African American 1 Asian American 10 Latino 4 White	13 African American 8 Latino 1 Middle Eastern

demographics and tracks of the seven participating classrooms. In two of the three schools, the students in the study classrooms mirrored the demographics of the school at large. In Jill Tenney's U.S. II classes in Allwood High School and Kevin Brooks' classrooms at Surrey High School, students more or less reflected the racial/ethnic breakdown of the rest of the school population. Bob Banks' classrooms had more African American and Latino students and fewer White students than his school as a whole, reflecting the demographics of racially and socioeconomically polarized Oak Knoll's lowest track. Jill Tenney's students were in a college preparatory track, although not in the highest track in the school, and Kevin Brooks' students were grouped together specifically because of their need for special education support in social studies. This distribution provided us with an exciting opportunity to consider the possibilities and challenges of implementing the new approach with a wide variety of students.

All three participating teachers had three to six years of teaching experience and were committed to the civic learning purposes of social studies education. Jill Tenney at Allwood High School, a White woman in her late twenties, entered a career in teaching through an alternate route program connected to a local state college. Upon completing her undergraduate studies in political science, Jill Tenney was uncertain which career path she would follow. Coaching softball at a local high school, an interest in politics and current events, and growing up in a family of educators convinced her that social studies education was an intriguing career option. Through her alternate route experiences in her own classroom and in education courses at the local college, Jill quickly realized the kind of teacher that she wanted to become. She reflected in an interview:

> By having the teachers that I had in high school who were very lecture-oriented, I knew that that's what I didn't want to be. Right off the bat I knew that . . . I didn't want to just stand up there, and stand behind a podium, and talk for forty five minutes . . . I didn't think that was helping anyone learn anything.

Memories of the lack of discussion in her own high school classes and her corresponding apathetic response convinced her that there were far better ways to engage students in the study of history, current events, and political issues.

In her fifth year of teaching at the time of the study, Jill's conviction that "whoever's doing the talking is doing the learning" motivated her to integrate various discussion and cooperative learning methodologies into her classroom. She believed that, because of this, her students "are engaged. I think they enjoy the class . . . enjoy being able to talk to each other because they never get an opportunity to do that" in other classes. Moreover, she was convinced that students are more active learners and learn more when they are challenged to come up with answers themselves, and are required to think critically and to perform more than the memorization of facts so often forgotten after the next assessment. To this end, one of Jill's goals as teacher "is to make social studies more relevant to the students' lives, and that was always one of my main purposes . . . I want them to think for themselves what America should do or what they should do." Jill's teaching philosophy and vested interest in developing civically active students was especially critical considering the ethnically and socioeconomically diverse student body represented in her classroom.

Bob Banks, Oak Knoll High School teacher, entered teaching through a Masters of Arts in Teaching program at a public university. Having majored in film and minored in history as an undergraduate, Bob was always interested in telling stories. For Bob, a White man in his late twenties, teaching history was just another way of telling the stories of the past. He claims he truly learned how to teach in the same way that soldiers learn how to be part of the Armed Forces: basic training. "It's coming in and . . . breaking me down and building me back up," he stated during an interview with the research team. Learning to teach, in other words, comes with the act of teaching itself, and requires continuing self-reflection and a willingness to implement new methods, organization, or other changes into your classroom.

Bob began his teaching career at Oak Knoll High School, and five years later, at the time of the study, he remained a U.S. history teacher there. He believed that a prerequisite to being a great teacher was treating your students like human beings, and allowing them to see that you, too, are a person with thoughts, feelings, and interests outside of schools. As Bob said,

> I see so many teachers that are like, I don't want to say robotic, per se, but . . . they're almost afraid of the kids. I see teachers that sort of talk down to

the kids . . . And it's just like . . . they're humans . . . You crack a joke, you let them know who you are. You get in there.

His belief in building relationships with all of his students was quickly evident to anyone who observed his classroom. An important aspect of this included making content relevant to students' lives. To this end, Bob focused on helping the students build clear connections between the past and the present and, whenever possible, explicitly tying current events into the history content of the course.

Kevin Brooks at Surrey High School, an African American man in his late twenties, began his work in education as a substitute in a middle and high school in the Surrey school district. Kevin majored in history in college; after receiving his emergency teacher certification to stay on at Surrey High School he felt immediately comfortable with the course content, but a bit shaky with regards to pedagogy. Like Bob, Kevin believed he truly learned how to teach through his first-hand experience in the classroom. As a new teacher, he felt that, like many educators, he "held tight" to the textbook and was hesitant to lead classroom discussions or other activities that deviated from the text. In his third year of teaching at the time of the study, he had " learn[ed] to leave the book alone a little bit," setting aside the textbook as a security blanket, and branching out in terms of methodology and creating varied classroom activities.

Kevin realized that his pedagogy and methods of assessment should vary in accordance with the diversity in the skills levels and types of learners in his classroom. However, working at a school in one of the poorest cities in the nation, he said he often had trouble getting his students engaged and willing to open up to new activities, especially when it came to cooperative learning. Kevin felt that for his students, who lived in an impoverished, often violent and unsafe community, "simple school, just academic stuff, it's just hard to grasp," and it was often difficult for them to understand the importance of schooling. Nevertheless, he was able to reach out to his students by consistently "trying to make [his class as] interesting as possible" and by relating the course content to his students' own experiences. Not only did this help increase student motivation and engagement, Kevin reflected, it also sent students the message that they, too, had knowledge worthy of being shared with the group. Kevin lived in Surrey and understood the daily challenges his students faced in this violent and impoverished setting, and he strongly desired to help his students see and use education as a means of improving their lives. His deep commitment was felt by his students, who spoke highly of Kevin and counted him among their few adult allies in the school.

The Plan of the Book

Making Citizens is structured around the curricular and pedagogical changes that Jill Tenney, Bob Banks, and Kevin Brooks implemented at Allwood, Oak Knoll, and Surrey High Schools. Each chapter weaves the scholarly literature on a particular aspect of the curricular and pedagogical transformation at the three schools together with data and findings from the study to present a picture of how that aspect of the civic learning approach could be integrated into the reader's own classroom. This first, introductory chapter focused on establishing the theoretical and empirical grounding for transforming social studies instruction and introduced the communities, schools, teachers, and students.

Chapter 2 of the book, *Essentially Different*, describes and illustrates how a thematic organization and essential questions can be used to reshape the traditional social studies curriculum. The chapter presents students' and teachers' experiences with the transformed curriculum, providing an overview of the themes and essential questions used by Kevin and Jill in their classrooms. Delving into the research on this topic, it illuminates both the theoretical justification for and the practical aspects of using themes and questions to improve civic learning. Chapter 2 sets the stage for the following four chapters which describe the civic learning strands linked to these themes and questions.

Chapter 3 of the book, *Talking Civics*, illustrates how discussion can be used to powerful effect in the U.S. History classroom to build students' speaking and listening capacities and promote an engaged orientation toward civic issues. The chapter presents three distinct forms of discussion—Socratic seminar, civil conversation, and Take-a-Stand—in detail, with special attention to how to integrate discussion throughout the curriculum in a way that builds students' abilities and connects history to local and current civic issues in a meaningful and authentic manner. These ideas are illustrated with examples from the three schools and the reflections of both students and teachers on their experiences with discussion.

Chapter 4, *Civic Communications*, focuses on the use of written and oral expression in the study classrooms to build civic and literacy skills and more deeply engage students with civic questions. This chapter describes how daily journal prompts, essays, persuasive speeches, debates, mock news conferences, and presentations can be used to meaningfully interweave the U.S. History curriculum and students' daily civic experiences. Lively examples from the classroom and content analysis of students' written work demonstrate how the process of building students' expressive skills promotes engagement and civic learning.

Chapter 5, *Beyond "Current Events Fridays,"* focuses on how consideration of current events, a mainstay of traditional social studies classrooms, can be taken out of the "current events Fridays" format and integrated into every unit and topic throughout the year. In the three classrooms, essential questions were the pivot that connected the past to the present, allowing students to bring their own concerns and ideas to discussion of ongoing dilemmas in U.S. history, such as who is an American and when should America go to war. This chapter highlights students engaging with current issues, amid the framework of a transformed U.S. History curriculum.

Chapter 6, *What's the Problem?*, explores the place of civic action research in the U.S. History classroom. It follows students at the three focal schools as they investigate the civic problems they selected (i.e. drugs, murder, racial profiling, no backpacks allowed in the hallway), describing how youth participatory action research approaches can be adapted for integration into a year-long social studies curriculum. The comparison among the students' experiences at the three schools highlights both the promise and complexity of action research in diverse settings.

Building upon the work of researchers who argue that larger social forces affect young people's emerging senses of themselves as civic beings, *Making Citizens* describes an approach to social studies education centered on making connections between the curriculum and what young people *do* know about civic life from their daily experiences as citizens, rather than the more common objective of "filling in" what they *do not* know. It is possible for social studies teachers to integrate meaningful civic learning into their classrooms. Moreover, this can be accomplished while enhancing student engagement, building desirable skills, and making the study of history and civic issues relevant to diverse students. This book describes how this can be done, providing clear, richly illustrated instruction on how teachers can reshape their social studies curricula and integrate key pedagogies to enhance students' civic learning and identity development. If we truly believe that civic learning occurs in social studies classrooms, that they are key places were citizens are "made," it is time to structure those classrooms with meaningful civic learning in mind.

2

ESSENTIALLY DIFFERENT

Using Essential Questions and Themes for Civic Learning

I am recommending that we begin to shape our presentation of American history around the question, "What does it mean to be an American, that is, a citizen of the United States?"

(Degler, 1987, p. 12)

The really big one was "What is an American?" You know . . . that was the basis of the course. It's a big question, "What makes an American?"

(Vincent, Allwood High School)

Students' Experiences of Social Studies Curriculum and Instruction

As noted in the previous chapter, students are more apt to describe their social studies classrooms as boring, repetitive, and focused on the details of the past than as meaningful spaces for civic learning. Unfortunately, this observation is not new. Consider the following interview excerpt from a study conducted over two decades ago (Cervone, 1983, p. 163):

Question: Have you ever heard the phrase "History repeats itself"?
Student: I think so. Isn't that when in the third grade they teach you about the Pilgrims, and then again in the fifth grade they talk about the Pilgrims, and then in eighth grade history you begin again with the Pilgrims?

In addition to repeatedly studying the same events, students in Cervone's study concurred that history, as they had learned it in school, was boring and irrelevant to their lives, "an endless series of dates, names, facts, and events to be learned and re-learned" (p. 164). Other educational research bears this out. Decades of data reveal that the most frequent instructional methods in social studies classrooms are lecture, worksheet completion, rote memorization, and test and quiz taking (Adler, 1991; Engle, 1996; Goodlad, 1983; Gross, 1952; Weiss, 1978). Furthermore, as noted in the last chapter, these methods, so ineffective for meaningful civic learning, seem to occur more prevalently in the poorest schools (Kahne & Middaugh, 2008).

Students in our study, when discussing their social studies classes from previous years, described a pedagogy that exactly reflected these decades of social studies research. Across the three schools, student after student depicted a social studies centered on bookwork and lecture. Said Omar in Surrey, "All we did was watch movies, hand out dittos." Narciso, from the same school, described a previous social studies class in which "teachers just give you the book, read out of it, do the work, that's it." Hope put a finer point on it, proclaiming "The teachers don't teach . . . they'll give us a worksheet and we'll have to read it and then just answer the questions." We heard similar reports from Allwood, where student Tariq reported that in previous classes "It was more like the teacher you know, it was the teacher teaching and the students taking notes." Janet compared the study year with past experiences, saying "This class with their projects with the entire curriculum is new. I'm used to like book work . . . Freshman year was just like out of the book, all taking notes." Katherine described earlier approaches as "'Here's the book,'" and Vincent said those classes were "just basically a lecture the whole time." In Oak Knoll, Veronica reported, similarly, that in the past "we just did bookwork. And worksheets."

Such methods reflect the notion that the core of social studies learning is student accumulation of the facts and sequence of history, with the textbook as the primary organizational tool. This approach implicitly posits knowledge as "a series of facts to be learned rather than as an opportunity to raise questions and confront societal or historical problems" (Caron, 2004, p. 4). When history is framed in this manner, note Bloom and Ochoa, teaching proceeds "as if there are simple answers to the questions we have about the nature of society, or worse . . . without asking those questions for which there are no answers" (1996, p. 327). Beyond the consistent reports of boredom from students, such a framework does not allow for students to ponder Vincent's "big question[s]," to grapple with the enduring civic issues so central to civic learning.

This chapter focuses on how the study team used themes and essential questions to put students' encounters with "really big" questions at the center of the curriculum. It considers the theoretical and empirical rationales for such an approach, describes how the approach was developed, and provides a sample from the curriculum. The chapter uses examples from classroom life to show readers how students and teachers engaged with this new curriculum that was based on the design principles for meaningful civic learning in diverse settings outlined in Box 1.1 on page 9 of the introductory chapter.

Themes and Essential Questions to Improve Social Studies Learning

The National Council for Social Studies asserts that social studies teaching and learning should "develop new understanding through a process of active construction of knowledge" (NCSS Curriculum Standards, 2009) and social studies scholars have advocated a more student-centered approach for decades. Scores of useful methods books suggest various approaches to promoting active learning in social studies classrooms. However pedagogical changes, as critical as they may be (and, indeed, the bulk of this book is devoted to exploring such changes), are not sufficient for constructing a social studies that promotes meaningful civic learning. If we hope to connect the historical study that dominates high school social studies both to students' lives and to larger civic issues, the shape and format of the curriculum must be reconsidered.

A number of social studies researchers suggest that a thematically organized curriculum—one that is arranged around major issues and questions rather than a strictly chronological sequence—can effectively address the problem of boring, repetitive, and irrelevant historical instruction and move social studies learners to a deeper understanding of themselves and the world. Such an approach can improve social studies instruction by helping teachers get to present-day issues and concerns sooner, making the curriculum more relevant to students' lives, allowing them to go more into depth, and facilitating an understanding of issues rather than memorization of isolated facts (Caron, 2004; Connor, 1997; White, 1995).

Essential questions—fundamental, debatable questions—can also serve to connect the present to the past and engage students in ongoing civic debates (Lattimer, 2008; Wiggins & McTighe, 1998). Lattimer describes essential questions as those which "get to the heart of the discipline," that "have more than one reasonable answer," that "connect the past to the present," and that "require regular reflection . . . in light of new information and ideas" (pp. 327–8). Wiggins and McTighe see such questions as "doorways to understanding" that help to "take a mass of content knowledge and shape it to engage and focus student inquiry" (p. 26).

Questions help both students and teachers to find the meaning beneath disparate activities, lessons, and chunks of content. Victor, quoted at the beginning of the first chapter, drew upon one of the essential question of the Social Change theme (described later in this chapter) to form and articulate a significant insight into the nature of civic action. He reflected,

> one of the essential questions whenever we took a test was . . . "Who has the ability to make change?" and I think, and you know, people. The general public has an ability, you know, they have the ability to make a change. We as the public, we can change things. We, we have the power to change. We can change.

In terms of civic learning, essential questions can get at the enduring civic issues that lie beneath the history-oriented curriculum and can provide students with the opportunity to make connections across time and place as they grapple with these large, fundamental questions.

There are many ways to approach thematic teaching and essential questions, ranging from the study of a narrowly defined historical period undergirded by a framing question, such as examining the Roman Empire while asking "What makes an empire great?" (Caron, 2004, p. 18), to more a more broadly constructed theme such as "The Rise and Fall of Empires" in which students "study empires from different periods to determine what factors led to their formation, their rise, and their decline" (White, 1995, p. 162). While the themes described above are historical in nature, the questions do not lend themselves to investigation of civic issues. This chapter will describe themes and questions that connect directly with ongoing social and civic problems and issues, themes and questions that help social studies meet its civic purposes by shifting it away from an unwavering historical focus.

These ideas are not new. In the early part of the 20th century, the 1916 Committee on Social Studies suggested that high school seniors take a course called "Problems of Democracy" designed to focus study on pressing issues and problems in American life (Nelson, 1994). In the 1930s and 1940s progressive educators advocated for a similar approach, based on the study of issues and problems, that would "educate students for the responsibilities of thoughtful and participatory citizenship' (Caron, 2004, p. 4). In the 1996 *Handbook on Teaching Social Issues* published by the National Council for the Social Studies, Evans, Newmann, and Saxe described an "issues-centered education" that "focuses on problematic questions that need to be addressed and answered" (in Evans & Saxe, 1996, p. 2). Issues-centered curricula, they explained, emphasize understanding over coverage; are connected by a thematic, disciplinary, interdisciplinary, or historical structure; build upon challenging content; and allow students a say in the inquiry process. Ochoa-Becker proclaimed in the introduction to the *Handbook* that "an issues-centered curriculum offers the greatest promise for improving citizen participation and the quality of democratic life in this society" (Evans & Saxe, 1996, p. ix).

New understandings of learning in general and civic learning in particular make this approach timelier than ever. As described in the previous chapter, a situated understanding of civic learning holds that what is available to be learned shapes learner identity itself. In other words, the design of the curriculum and the nature of classroom practices shape students' understandings of learning and their sense of themselves as learners. Applied to social studies learning, an approach in which questions are immediately answerable (e.g. "What were the three causes of World War I?"), invokes a fundamentally different sort of knowledge than an approach based on large, open questions (e.g. "When should the United States intervene in the affairs of other countries?"). In the former, knowledge is discrete and bounded; history is concluded, memorizable, fixed. In the latter, knowledge is open, under construction, subject to analysis; history is still under discussion.

Consider the remarks of Janet from Allwood High as she reflected upon the difference between her first two, chronologically organized years of social studies instruction and the new, thematic approach she has just experienced (emphasis added):

> I could say freshman year it was World History. *There's not much you can give an opinion on because what's happened has happened.* Last year, unfortunately it was U.S. I, *so it's still what happened has happened already.* Like we can maybe disagree or something but *it's not like we can have a really open discussion with how it affects us.*

According to Janet's perspective, her World History and U.S. I courses were places where "what's happened has happened." History and, by extension, historical study, as presented in those classrooms, was over, completed. Janet saw a direct connection between the completed quality of history, as experienced in those classrooms, and her and her classmates' ability to connect with the past, to "have a really open discussion with how it affects us." As knowledge is differently constructed, so are learners' understandings of the nature of social studies itself. In Janet's first two years of high school she experienced a social studies in which learners memorized past events and considered issues that were presented as resolved. History was a spectator sport or, more accurately, a chore to be completed. In their year studying U.S. history with Jill Tenney, as I will illustrate below, students became part of an ongoing civic conversation, an "open discussion" that connected the past to the present and to their lives, making historical learning a more active and vibrant endeavor.

If we consider the typology of civic identity described in Table 1.1 in Chapter 1, we can see how students' sense of themselves as citizens also takes place amid the nested contexts of classroom, school, and community. Themes and questions can help students draw connections between these three levels. For example, during the Conflict and Resolution theme, students in Surrey High School took part in a "Socratic seminar" based on the late 18th-century Edmund Burke quote "All that is necessary for the triumph of evil is that good men do nothing." They discussed violence in their community in relation to historical conflicts, pondering the obligation of the individual to stand up against evil. Kevin Brooks explained,

> I mean from a student's standpoint you know, especially the group of kids I have, learning about Reconstruction is not a priority to them, alright, but they see now, actually see these things happening in real life. The things we're discussing, they can see it and I think they can relate to it and are a lot more willing to make the connections.

This seminar allowed students to consider, in the context of historical study, issues that had tremendous impact on their daily lives. In this way, a thematic approach combined with essential questions can produce transformational shifts in how students understand their relationship to both history and civic life.

The rest of this chapter explores how the curriculum was created by the research team and experienced by students and teachers in the classroom.

Creating the Curriculum

If students find social studies frustrating, so do teachers. On the first day of the summer workshop, Jill, Bob, and Kevin articulated their goals as social studies educators. The discussion, without prodding, naturally shifted to the frustrations that each teacher experienced daily. Kevin Brooks, teaching special education social studies at an urban high school, indicated that his goals extended "far beyond the social studies domain." He reflected on the problems with which his students entered his classroom each day and suggested that he felt obligated to teach in a way that validated these experiences, while also assisting his students as they navigated these dilemmas. He felt that the textbook they used was not useful for the type of social studies he wanted his students to experience, saying "I wish it were more thematic but schools haven't evolved." Jill Tenney noted that she was most frustrated by her students "not understanding the diversity of the United States. Their worldview is so limited." Bob Banks felt that "skills should be emphasized over content. I want my students to develop the skills to support their arguments with research." He felt that his students' extracurricular responsibilities including employment and childcare often stood in the way from their focus on school work.

These three teachers' yearnings for a more skill-based, thematic, and meaningful social studies curriculum made them enthusiastic about the four design principles undergirding this project. Jill liked the principles yet was apprehensive about her district supporting them. She noted, "We have quarterly exams that are aligned to the district curriculum and that curriculum is *far* more traditional than these goals." Bob said that he was "free to do these things in his district. We have a curriculum but the skills are emphasized over the content." Kevin was the most enthusiastic about the design principles, saying "I feel like schools are often very adversarial to students. This sort of approach would be different."

Kevin and Jill believed strongly that to achieve the design principles, their U.S. II curricula would have to be reorganized so that students could grapple with big issues and questions. They felt the chronologically organized curriculum was an impediment to drawing links between historical content, contemporary issues, and students' issues and concerns. They were also committed to covering the content required by their district. To this end, each teacher brought his or her school's standard curriculum to the summer workshop and, working together with a consulting historian, the research team brainstormed innovative ways to teach important historical content in a meaningful and conceptual manner that could tap into students' civic experiences. Bob participated whole-heartedly in this enterprise, although he was not sure that he wanted to completely upend his approach to a course he felt he had taught successfully for several years.

The exercise of organizing content into themes was a struggle at times, with each teacher having slightly different opinions of essential historical content. For instance, the suburban sprawl of the 1950s was meaningful content to one teacher, but not to another. Another felt that civic literacy such as the donkey symbolizing the Democratic Party and the elephant symbolizing the Republican Party was very important. Each teacher had a different starting point for his or her chronologically organized U.S. History II course. Kevin was supposed to teach from the *Reconstruction* period through the present. Bob's curriculum began with the *Gilded Age* and continued through the present. Jill's school required a brief unit on economics before plunging into chronological history beginning with *World War I*. These differences created some complications, but they also highlighted the constructed nature of all history curricula.

Drawing upon the "understanding by design" approach advocated by Wiggins and McTighe (1998), the team began to rethink how to approach historical content. The consulting historian suggested that "Instead of 'covering' the 1920s merely because it's in the book, try to think of ways to *use* the 1920s to teach about a particular theme." What began as a one-day effort to "pick some questions to go throughout the curriculum" turned into a multi-day affair in which each teacher laid out all aspects of his or her previous year's curriculum for collective reshaping. A dynamic and energetic process ensued whereby all members of the research team highlighted, circled, and categorized similarly themed content. Team members shared their categories, provided a rationale for their choices, and, with discussion and reconciliation, developed emerging themes supported by each teacher.

The teachers decided that five themes, the first two sharing a quarter and the remaining three lasting one marking period each, would be the optimal way to organize content: *Government, Economics, Conflict and Resolution, Movement of People,* and *Social Change*. The teachers' hope was that each of these themes would scaffold students' understandings of U.S. history so that after 180 school days, all students would be in a position to effectively grapple with the open-ended course question, "What is an American?," a question with strong potential to bridge civics, history, and students' own lives and concerns. Table 2.1 depicts the themes, essential questions, and basic content developed during the workshop.

The three teachers varied in their adherence to the curriculum described in Table 2.1. At Allwood High School, Jill Tenney followed the framework throughout the year, organizing her teaching and assessment around the themes and essential questions developed during the summer workshop. She was able to teach the entire curriculum, developing numerous lessons and activities for each theme. Kevin Brooks also followed the thematic, question-centered approach although, drawn deeply into the civic action project described in Chapter 5 of this book and challenged by his students' literacy skills and poor attendance, he did not get

TABLE 2.1 Themes and Essential Questions for Meaningful Civic Learning in Diverse Settings

Theme	Government	Economics	Conflict and resolution	Movement of people	Social change
Overarching Question			WHAT IS AN AMERICAN?		
Essential Questions	What purpose does government serve? What is a good American citizen? Am I a good American citizen?	What do Americans owe each other? Why are some rich and some poor? Is the American economy fair?	What is America's role in the world? Why does the U.S. go to war? When should it? Can nations cooperate?	Who is an American? Why do people come to America? How do different groups define their American identities?	Are all Americans equal? How do Americans make social change? Who has the power to make change? Do you? What forces shape society?
Content (not inclusive)	Branches of government Nature of democracy Federal system Political ideology Bureaucracy, institutions Electoral politics Civic participation	Basic terms Capitalism: stock market, Great Depression, industrialization Role of government Economic reforms World economy Personal economics	WWI WWII Cold War Vietnam, Korean Wars Middle East Gulf War, Iraq, War on Terror Genocide	Immigration Migration: Native Americans, African Americans, Japanese internment, Puerto Ricans Contemporary challenges: Deurbanization, suburbanization, gentrification, globalization	Race/Civil rights movement Latino rights movement Gender/Women's rights movement Social protest

through all five themes. Bob Banks chose to stay with a chronological approach, aiming to integrate the themes and questions when appropriate. This provided a natural experiment of the efficacy of a thematic approach versus a chronological approach with thematic intentions, as will be discussed later in this chapter.

Sample Theme and Questions: Social Change

The sample theme of Social Change, shown in Table 2.2, was developed by the research team in the summer workshop and fleshed out during the school year by Jill Tenney. This theme, like most of the others, lasted for a school quarter (the exception being Government and Economics, which shared a quarter). Within each theme there were discrete units, held together by the essential questions that undergirded the entire theme. As Danny, an Allwood student, put it,

> social change. That was, that was always the kind of, the kind of theme in the background. Like, alright, like there was the Latino movement . . . and the feminist movement, it had social change, that was always in the back. Always in the back.

Table 2.2 illustrates the interweave of theme, units, questions, discussion, and assignments in the curricular approach.

The final assessment for this theme was an essay test in which students considered the unit's essential questions, drawing upon content from the units to answer fundament questions about social change.

Student Learning with Themes and Questions

Although they lacked a sophisticated language to describe the approach and struggled to articulate the impact of a realigned historiographic framework, Allwood and Surrey students were aware that something was different about U.S. history during the study year, referring to the approach as "grouping the things that were alike together," "jumping around," and studying history "by theme." Students' responses echoed the experts' predictions: they described being able to reach deeper understandings of the materials, making connections across time, and relating history to their own lives.

"Better Maps" and "Heavy Information": A Deeper Understanding of History

Connor argues that "the primary benefit of teaching U.S. history thematically is that it affords a better grasp of the principal developments in the nation's history by treating issues in depth" (1997, p. 203). Or, as Allwood student Kristin put it,

TABLE 2.2 Social Change Theme with Essential Questions, Units, Content, and Sample Assignments

Essential Questions
- Are all Americans equal?
- How can/do Americans make social change?
- What other forces, other than individuals, shape society?
- Who has the power to make change? Do you?
- Is it ever okay to break the law? When?

Unit title	Content	Sample projects/assignments/discussions
Unit 1: African American Struggle for Rights	Reconstruction, Amendments, KKK, White citizens; Birth of a Nation, Freedman's Bureau, Black codes, Jim Crow, Plessy, WEB Dubois/Booker T. Washington, NAACP/Marcus Garvey, Segregation/Integration of the Armed Forces, Brown vs. Board, Montgomery bus boycott, MLK/Malcolm X, Civic Rights Act, Voting rights, Freedom Riders, Civil rights movement, Black Panthers, Jackie Robinson, Black Power movement	Newscast reporting on a moment in civil rights history.
Unit 2: Latino Struggle for Rights	Braceros, United Farm Workers, Cesar Chavez, Bilingual education, Immigration rights/who is an American, English only	Carousel on Latino social protest movements.
Unit 3: Women's Struggle for Rights	Women's suffrage movement; Seneca Falls Convention; Susan B. Anthony; Elizabeth Cady Stanton; Margaret Sanger; 19th Amendment; 1920s' flappers; Mary McLeod Bethune; Women and the home front during WWII; 1950s; Betty Friedan; Gloria Steinem; E.R.A.; Roe vs. Wade; Title IX; Labor issues	Jigsaw on women's rights from Seneca Falls to the present. Comparison of primary documents from the 1950s. "Take-A-Stand" on Title IX.
Unit 4: Social Protest	This unit is devoted to the individualized social protest projects and presentations.	Social Protest Project: Students prepare a four-minute presentation and display describing a social protest of the 20th or 21st century. The project must answer the essential questions and consider why this social protest is important in a democracy. It should include a KWL chart and at least four images.

"I like it better when it's jumping around just because of the fact that I think it makes it easier for us to learn . . . sometimes the topics will overlay from the past . . . and then when you go back, you kind of interlock what was missed and understand it better." Similarly, Rebecca struggled initially with the approach, but in the end saw it as a way of getting beyond "just trying to remember a timeline in my head." The approach "actually gave me a *better map of history* in the end," she concluded. This sense of developing a "better map of history" was echoed by classmates, who described how this year they were able to see the links between historical events in a new way, getting at the concepts beneath the events. It was, noted Allwood student Kristin, a good way for "us to develop the skills of learning history."

Kevin's students, like Jill's, spoke of big underlying concepts—"heavy information," in Omar's words—that they would "always remember when you get out of school." Comparing Kevin's teaching to other teachers, Omar explained,

> Like he teach more, he teach more than most of my other teachers. Nothing wrong, they do teach but he teach like he give you information that you need . . . when you get out of school. He gives you *heavy information* that you will always remember when you get out of school. Other teachers, they give you information but it won't be as heavy as his though.

"Heavy information," for Omar, meant memorable concepts that he felt were worth learning and incorporating into his intellectual repertoire.

In the economics unit one of the framing questions was "Is the American economy fair?" Kevin had students write on which economic system they preferred and which they saw as more fair. Omar described how he felt about studying these topics.

> Like he was telling us about . . . capitalism and Communism. I never knew that about capitalism and Communism until he brought it up. Now I'm going to remember that through my whole year, my whole year I will remember that. If I have kids, I'll explain Communism and capitalism and everything else.

Omar's experience demonstrates how encountering abstract concepts within a thematic, question-based framework makes them more meaningful, and therefore more memorable.

"We Can Always Compare It to What We've Learned": Connections Across Time

The thematic organization and essential questions worked together to help students relate discrete events to larger themes. In Allwood, as shown in Table 2.2, the students studied social change through shifting temporal and group perspectives that allowed students to see critical connections between time periods. As Robbie described,

> I always knew what was going on . . . And I think it's good that we learned it by theme, because we can always compare it to what else we've learned. So you can kind of see how situations, even though they're fifty years apart, are kind of the same. So when you do it all by like, I don't know, social change, and you see the women's rights movement is the same as the civil rights movement, basically, it really, it just helps you see things and understand things a lot better.

For Robbie, study of the women's movement and the civil rights movement took place amid a larger discussion of the struggle for equal rights and the place of social action in the United States that undergirded the Social Change theme. Similarly, during the Economics theme, students discussed the concept of a "war economy" from the World Wars to Vietnam, and through the recent conflicts in Iraq and Afghanistan.

During the Conflict and Resolution theme, students considered the big questions of "What is America's role in the world?", "Why does the U.S. go to war? When should it?" and "Can nations cooperate?" as they studied conflicts from the World Wars through Iraq and Afghanistan. Students were discussing the conflicts in Vietnam and Iraq in November, a radical departure from chronological approaches in which classes frequently do not get through the 1960s. This ability to "get to the present" will be described in detail in Chapter 5, *Beyond "Current Events Fridays."* Connor notes that "A common problem in many high school U.S. history courses is the neglect of teaching about the recent past. It is not uncommon to hear of classes that never get to the civil rights movement or the Vietnam War, much less the events of recent decades" (1997, p. 204). A thematic approach allows "frequent opportunities for discussing contemporary issues within an historical framework" and, excitingly, "students can be holding informed discussions of the views of our political leaders on current issues by mid-October" (p. 204).

Students appreciated how the thematic approach allowed them to see the connections between the different time periods, providing a fundamentally different interpretation of the adage "history repeats itself" from that expressed by the student quoted at the very start of this chapter. This approach made key topics, in Tariq's words, "hard to forget." He illustrated this notion using the second quarter Conflict and Resolution theme,

> The way that this differs . . . is that you get to relate more topics and these issues. Like we always learn like "this is 1920s, 1930s, 1940s, 1960s," and by the time you get to the '70s, you're like "what happened in the '30s?" But

this is all like "OK, World War II this happened. And so did this and so did that." Then you skip around 'til like Vietnam and this happened. Then you go back to like World War I and like the way she used to talk she was like "remember what happened in World War I? With that whole issue? Well now it's happening in World War II. Remember what happened in World War II? Now it's happening in Vietnam." She would always relate these topics that we'd be like it's really hard to forget. Like you wouldn't forget unless you really tried hard to forget.

Tariq found that staying with an issue across time made historical study more memorable.

Samara agreed, calling the thematic approach "easier" than a chronological approach,

> because sometimes [in past years] you'd be at peace, and all of the sudden you'd go to war. So we had a whole war section, and we had a whole civil rights movement, and I like that . . . it was easier. You weren't going from topic to topic, and you weren't just like learning something new one semester and then learning something crazy different.

As Connor notes, the "repetition" found in thematic learning helps students make sense of the material (1997, p. 204).

For Jill, essential questions were the key tool that allowed her to draw links across time. She pushed students to continually consider the essential questions by making them central to final assessments. Jill described this strategy at a research team meeting,

> Every test, we give them the same questions. But they have to answer the questions in relation to the unit they just had. So is war just? Is war just in World War I? Is war just in World War II? Is war just in Cold War? Is war just in the Middle East? Is war just with genocide where we didn't go to war necessarily in Darfur or anything like that so they had to answer the same essential question over and over again in respect to different time periods and now hopefully after the take a stand, they'll be able to kind of connect that and really weigh is war just? Should America take action or inaction knowing all the different time periods that they did or didn't.

She used the essential questions in her unit exams, asking students to draw upon their new knowledge as they grappled with these enduring issues.

"It's About Everything": Connections Beyond the Classroom

White argues that "history teachers must consider the relationship between content and learners" and that "connecting subject matter to the experiences of students is a constant challenge" for teachers of the subject (1995, p. 160). Themes and questions provided space for students to link the curriculum to their own lives. Surrey student Omar drew upon what he had learning in the Conflict and Resolution theme to describe how he would advise a new student at his high school. He drew upon the underlying issues and questions of the theme to make sense of life for youth in violent Surrey, explaining,

> My advice to them is stay out of trouble and do your best for all four years. Stay out of trouble and try not to [get involved in] none of that nonsense or violence . . . Like Mr. Brooks said, Cold War is like you talking, saying like "I might have fight with a boy." [saying] He'd like to punch him in his face and stuff like that. But the *hot war* he said, he said the hot war is when we actually physical fighting like punching really, really fighting and punching each other and stuff like that . . . And I seen that and I seen that going on a lot here too.

Advising the fictitious newcomer to Surrey to stay out of the "hot war," mind his own business, and stay out of trouble, Omar makes a seemingly unlikely but resonant connection between a historical period that predates his birth and the situation of young people in Surrey. Similarly, in Allwood students taking part in a Socratic seminar on child labor during the Economics unit connected their experiences in their native countries to the moral and economic issue being studied. For the diverse, immigrant dense population of Allwood, this made the study of U.S. history relevant. As Samara noted, "This year it's more like, everything, and not just like Civil War, it's not just about U.S., it's about everything all over the world."

During the Conflict and Resolution theme, students participated in a Take-a-Stand discussion, in which they deliberated over whether or not they would be willing to fight in Iraq, as well as the justifications for the war and U.S. intervention more broadly. They considered statements like, "The land in present day Israel belongs to the Palestinians" and "If I were an Israeli I would want peace no matter what," placing themselves outside of their American identities and exploring conflicts that exist beyond the United States, but nevertheless affect it (and are affected by it). During the unit on genocide within this theme, students considered the global scope of citizenship, making presentations on genocidal events across time and place and delving into the issue of human and national responsibility for evil acts. In the context of transnationalism and globalization, themes and questions allowed students to traverse the boundaries of the United States and relate to the world as more than just Americans.

"We Never Came Up with a Finite Answer": Opening History to Interpretation

Themes and questions can fundamentally change how history is understood in classrooms that employ them fully. Framing a curriculum around large, unanswerable questions allowed Allwood and Surrey students to become part of an ongoing civic conversation, building an interpretive framework into the very structure of the course. As Rebecca at Allwood High put it,

> We had the essential questions on every test. Like what is a, well they changed throughout the year but I think the basic ones are "what is an American?" "Who can make change?" "What, who besides a group can make change?" "Can you make change?" There was a lot about changing the world. A lot about I think are all Americans equal? So those were things that we explored but never actually, we never came up with a finite answer. It was just let's try and figure this out together.

The questioning frame disallowed a single correct answer and made interpretation a critical, ongoing activity in these classrooms.

In classroom discussions, as will be described in detail in Chapter 3, *Talking Civics*, students grappled with enduring civic issues that had no ready answers. The following excerpt from a Take-a-Stand during the Conflict and Resolution theme demonstrates this idea. In this episode, the students were standing up in the front of the classroom. They arrayed themselves across the classroom on a continuum from "agree" to "disagree" in response to statements posed by the teacher. In this exchange, Jill has just made the statement "The U.S. should not intervene in foreign countries." The students rearranged themselves and began, unprompted, to discuss:

Annie: I'm on the fence because it depends on the circumstances. No reason [for us to go to war], then I'm against, but if it's some reason like terrorism, then yes.

Jack: We shouldn't intervene unless it affects us.

Tommy: We wouldn't have any allies if we didn't.

Danny: What allies do we have now? Don't we have only Britain? Don't we have like no allies?

Mary: It depends. Don't we want to help people from being abused?

Annie: If it's none of our businesses, everyone thinks we're the bad guys. Don't we have enough problems of our own? Then they'd just hate us more.

After grappling with the issue by expressing and rebutting both sides of the question, the debate on U.S. global responsibility was left open in two senses—it was a question without a finite answer, and, as such, it was also an approachable discussion in which students could become invested and form their own opinions.

In this open atmosphere, students were eager to press discussion forward. One student, after sharing her opinion during a Take-a-Stand, remarked "I didn't hear anything from that side of the room," and then directly asked her quiet classmate for his opinion, saying, "Like, Mohammed, what do you think?" In a setting in which neither text nor teacher were the ultimate authorities and where students' voices counted, students looked to one another to better understand the issues they confronted. Students' perspectives were positioned as valuable knowledge, and knowledge itself was understood to be co-constructed through "open discussion," as Janet put it earlier.

Essential questions allowed the teachers to balance content learning with this open approach to knowledge. Raman reflected,

> Every time we had tests we had to answer the open-ended questions. The ... I forgot what they're called but there's five of them ... Essential questions there we go. And they basically stayed the same throughout that chapter that we were dealing with, that pertained to it. It would have to pertain to it or change our answers to that like era. And they were the same questions so that was kind of fun and easy to do. Each time those different like facts I got to use.

Students were accountable for the "different facts" they "got to use," but the very nature of the questions used meant they needed to take part in an ongoing civic discourse on an unresolved issue. In Chapter 4, *Civic Communications*, we will look more closely at some of the written work that resulted from this approach.

Unanswerable questions could be frustrating. As Jill Tenney described,

> an essential question is something that they're critically thinking about and now we can compare things that are similar, they can critically think, and say, hmmm, what is the answer to this question? And it frustrates the hell out of them! ... And now they're like, ahh, I got to use my brain, and now even though it's frustrating and they express that, it's, they're learning. And they're thinking critically. And yeah, it's hard. And it's hard to think about these questions. There's no answer. And they expressed that many times. There's no answer to these questions, what's going on here? Especially in the beginning of the year. And they were very frustrated by the fact that, hey, wait a second, why am I getting a question here without an answer? Well, because, you know what, in life, there's not answers. And you have to think about it. And you have to form your own opinions with the knowledge that you have. And I think that we were able to do that in this kind of approach.

For Jill, the essential questions were a way to open the curriculum to discussion, questioning, and exploration, drawing students into some of the central debates in U.S. civic life.

Teacher Reflections

Retrenching the curriculum around themes and essential questions was a challenging task. Jill said it was,

> really kind of being a first year teacher again. Even though the content is still the same, it's taught in a different framework and a different manner, and you know just doing the research, and coming up with how I'm going to teach this, or whatever we're talking about, is, not frustrating, but just time consuming.

Despite the extra work, after a year teaching with this approach, Jill felt sure that the thematic approach and the essential questions were mutually interdependent. Although essential questions are frequently recommended by curriculum designers, and even written into some state curriculum standards that maintain a chronological approach, Jill felt the questions, good as they were, would have been useless within a chronological approach. "You cannot do an essential question with a chronological approach," she said, "because it just doesn't make sense." She explained further,

> you can ask, you know, "is social protest important to a democracy?" and you can cover it chronologically, but they're not going, they can't relate civil rights to women's rights, because women's rights, first of all, it's not even a topic. They talk about five different things that happened to change women's history, let's say, none of which are in the same time period and none of which connect, and there's no progression. They don't see the progression out of it. So therefore that's a loss. It's gone. Civil rights, same thing. They don't see the progression, so it's gone. You can't even relate a topic. And now, instead of working with five essential questions for a theme, you're working with 20 essential questions for the year. That's not meaningful. It's a loss . . . They lose the thread, and they cannot remember 20 questions. They can remember five.

To get students to engage deeply with questions that bridged history, contemporary issues, and personal experience, she felt the thematic organization made all the difference.

Kevin, teaching students with special needs at Surrey, moved more slowly through the curriculum during the implementation year, but he was enthusiastic about the thematic organization. "I loved it to no end," he said. "I think it's more streamlined and more easy to make things make a lot more sense. A whole lot more sense." He described how the Movement of People theme made more sense for his students than studying the various events related to immigration and migration whenever they happened to come up in the curriculum.

You're talking about the first great migration of Blacks from the South following the Civil War and now you're back to talking about it during World War I and now you're talking about, back talking about it after World War II. And there's the same like it's pretty much the same story again and again but these students are now able to see how the events that are taking place are leading to the same response. It's a lot easier to talk about immigration, Blacks from the South, it's a lot easier to talk about immigration from Eastern Europeans coming over because they're coming over and they're moving around for the same reasons. So students can understand that and grasp it but when it's broken up like here's the European immigration wave and blah-blah-blah and here's African-Americans migrating. We were talking about it in Black History Month, that sort of thing like it's so choppy.

Rather than fracturing the notion of migration into disparate pieces scattered across the curriculum, Kevin liked how he could ask his students to consider the larger issues behind migration with a thematic organization.

Similar thinking applied to his teaching of the Conflict and Resolution theme. Kevin explained,

I think it's a lot easier for students to see the cycle. How things changed and how they go back and how they change and go back in sort of a pattern. It's a lot easier to understand. I know I've never as clearly understood the Cold War and our United States aggression with Russia, I mean USSR until I approached it this way. It's a lot easier to see how events are happening in World War I or leading up to World War I, affect what happen following World War II. And I know if I'm understand that a lot better, and I'm a teacher, and I know the students are understanding a lot better. It's presented in a way like more of a story. And it's a lot easier to understand a story with a streamlined narrative and theme than when it is if someone is presenting you with something here and right now we're switching over to the gilded age and now we're talking about TR and all these sorts of stuff. It's really choppy, chronologically teaching history. I will never do that again.

Helping his students see the "story" of history was a strength of the approach for Kevin who, despite the lack of resources available at his school, preferred using a thematic organization rather than the chronologically organized textbook.

Both Jill and Kevin found the thematic approach to be critical to their desire to bridge historical and contemporary issues and students' own interests and experiences. Jill did not think it would be possible to enact the curriculum in a chronological manner, saying,

You cannot possibly connect it chronologically. You can't like, it's almost like you have all your topics, and you pull it through to the present, and you can't pull it through to the present chronologically. Because they, it's too long of a time lapse. How do you compare World War I to Vietnam when the time lapse is six months that you covered it, since you covered it? What kid is going to remember that? What student is going to remember that this happened in World War I? They're not, they're just not. Their time span of knowledge is very short, you know, to form the understanding. And there's no way you can cover something in the beginning in the year, and relate it to something at the end of the year. That's gone. It's gone! They don't know what they did last week! Let alone, you know, remembering in September what the themes were in World War I. They, you know, they would look at you like you had three heads. And that was happening in the past.

Kevin too felt passionately about this, saying,

after teaching chronologically and now teaching thematically, I will never teach chronologically again. Ever. Because it's chronological, it's presented so choppy. Like this is where it started, this problem started, this is where this problem ended and that was it. Until you see the same thing repeated . . . 40 years later that we didn't get, that we didn't cover within these two months. It is really so choppy.

Although neither Kevin nor Jill taught in a school or district that encouraged this approach to the history curriculum, both finished the project convinced they would never return to a chronologically organized approach.

Bob in Oak Knoll demurred from reorganizing the curriculum thematically, feeling more comfortable with the chronological organization he had always employed. In the summer workshop he expressed his belief that he could integrate the essential questions and themes throughout the curriculum without a thematic reorganization. However he found it difficult to integrate the essential questions and themes into the course and was frustrated at the end of the year by, yet again, not being able to "get past Jimmy Carter."

the only thing is, teaching the curriculum in a chronological manner like this district does, like this department does, it's such a time suck that I was really, really disappointed that I didn't get past Jimmy Carter. So disappointed. I swore to myself at the beginning of this year I'm going to get to Clinton and it just didn't happen.

Maintaining the chronological approach impeded Bob's ability to make contemporary connections throughout the curriculum—while Kevin and Jill were discussing the war in Iraq as early as November in the context of the Conflict and Resolution theme, Bob was unable to make it to the early 1980s by the end of the school year. This will be fully addressed in Chapter 5, *Beyond "Current Events Fridays."* Bob's decision to stick with a more familiar curricular organization, while completely understandable, had ramifications for the rest of his year.

In two of the three classrooms, then, a strong thematic approach was the weft though which the civics skills strands wove. It left its imprint on the civic learning experiences at the three schools that are documented in the chapters that follow this one. In two of the three classrooms, discussions and writing were based on essential questions, current events were framed by thematic units, and civic action was placed in the context of a civic question-oriented curriculum. The next four chapters will focus on the civic skills strands at the heart of the new approach.

Top Ten Recommendations for Using Themes and Questions

1. Create themes that touch on issues cutting through a number of historical time periods.
2. Create themes that have strong potential to relate to current-day issues.
3. Create themes that represent intellectually and socially significant issues from the history under study.
4. Create questions that are debatable and allow students to connect their own lives to history.
5. Choose questions that require students to have content knowledge to grapple with them effectively.
6. Choose questions that will interest/engage students.
7. Choose questions that are appropriately challenging for the students.
8. Choose few enough questions that students can remember them throughout the unit.
9. Return to questions repeatedly throughout the theme or unit, revisiting them with each new piece of knowledge.
10. Choose questions and themes that get at key civic dilemmas and thus will incorporate students into ongoing civic discourse.

3
TALKING CIVICS

Open Discussion in the
Social Studies Classroom

it was so much, like, open discussion that you thought you were just hanging
out with a bunch of friends . . . People are actually learning instead of taking
a nap or something.

(Tariq, Allwood High School)

everybody wants to have input on everything. And when it's time to leave,
everybody's still trying to talk about it. Trying not to leave. Mr. Brooks will
be like "OK, you all, we got to go."

(Tamika, Surrey High School)

Consider the last time you had a good conversation. Were you animated? Excited?
Involved? Did you reflect on something important to you? Articulate a long held
but not frequently said feeling? Reconsider a previously held conviction? Tell or
hear a story? Gain insight into someone else's perspective? Feel a sense of human
connection? Feel pierced by sadness or compassion? Recoil in disgust? Share a
moment of laughter and high spirits? Conversation flows throughout our days like
water and air. With family, friends, at work, in school hallways, in stores, on the
sidelines of sporting events, among parents watching children play in a local park,
humans interact through talk.

When asked what made for a "good discussion," students at Allwood, Surrey,
and Oak Knoll high schools captured these same notes of connection, authentic
exchange, and self-expression. "Yeah, it's fun, because people agree and other
people don't agree, so we just go back and forth till we all agree on one thing,"
said Narciso, a Surrey High student. "Time flies by," said Ryan from Allwood,
"and some people don't get what they want to say in, because you have so many
people that want to say something." "Keeping the conversation going," Amy from

Oak Knoll explained, describing a good discussion. "Laughing at what, like, the other person says." Student after student described good discussions as those with a natural flow, exchange of ideas, humor, animation, excitement, and interest.

Discussion enlivens any classroom. In social studies classrooms, discussion fulfills a variety of purposes, from buildings students' listening and public speaking competencies to serving as a means by which to connect the curriculum to students' own lives and to larger civic issues. This chapter considers the civic learning benefits of discussion in the classroom, meshing a review of research on discussion with an examination of the experiences of the students and teachers in the three study classrooms to better illustrate and explore the utility of discussion for helping to transform social studies classrooms into sites for meaningful civic learning.

In this chapter, I consider the overwhelming evidence for the efficacy of open discussion as a tool for encouraging civic awareness and engagement, grapple with the puzzle of why such discussion is so infrequently employed, and share the discussion experiences of the students and teachers in this study. I also put forward a plea for doing what we can to make classroom discussion mirror the satisfying, authentic exchanges that we enjoy beyond the classroom. Such discussions left indelible impressions on students, distinguishing the study classrooms from previous social studies experiences (and often from other classroom experiences as well). "Not allowing students to engage in open discussion on important issues and topics is the most detrimental intellectual void in schools" (Wolk, 2003, p. 103).

Why Discuss?

> simply requiring attention to politics and government is not enough to foster greater involvement among high school students. Instead, it is when students report that teachers encourage *open discussions* [emphasis added] about those matters that their scores on scales of civic behavior climb. This finding holds up even when other important influences are taken into account, which suggests that when teachers promote lively classroom participation, they are also encouraging involvement outside the classroom as well.
>
> *(Zukin et al., 2006, p. 142)*

What is "open discussion"? Dillon describes discussion as "a collaborative pursuit consisting of group talk over a common area of inquiry in which the participants are disposed to be open to a variety of points of view" (1994, p. 51). Cook and Tashlik (2004) see discussion as centered on open-ended questions without right or wrong answers that invite thoughtful, and often controversial, responses. Definitions vary, but researchers seem to agree that discussion involves the open exchange of ideas among a group of people, the same fundamental aspects of discussion that Zukin and his fellow researchers found to be so powerful for civic engagement.

At the study schools, almost 100% of the participating students (90–100% on each measure) agreed that they had discussions during the year of the project in which they could freely offer their opinions and in which many different opinions were expressed, that they had talked about racism, sexism, and discrimination, that they had talked about current events, and that it was "ok" in the classrooms both to disagree with the teacher and to hold opinions that were different from those held by peers.

Consider the following snippet of discussion from Allwood High. Kristi, Ms. Tenney's student teacher, led a Take-a-Stand discussion (much more on this discussion format later) to wrap up the Conflict and Resolution section of the course for her "level one" (college prep, but not honors) class. The class had 19 students, two African American, three Arab American, five White, and nine Asian American (including East and South Asian heritage students). The students had reached the end of the Conflict and Resolution theme, having studied the World Wars, the Korean War, the Vietnam War, the Cold War, the first Gulf War, and the current conflict in the Middle East, and were engaging in a wrap up discussion using one of the three formats we developed for the project.

"We're going to play 'Take-a-Stand,'" announces Kristi.

A ripple of excitement passes through the classroom. Students begin to stand and push the desks toward the back of the room. On one wall the teacher has put a sign saying "Agree," on the opposite wall a sign marked "Disagree."

"The United States should not intervene in foreign countries," Kristi states loudly.

Students move past each other, arranging themselves as the front of the room on a continuum from "agree" to "disagree." The distribution is fairly even. Annie, an African American girl standing in between the two extremes, starts things off saying, "I'm on the fence, because it depends on the circumstances. No reason [for us to go to war], then I'm against it, but if it's some reason, like terrorism, then yes."

Jack, a White boy standing slightly more toward the "disagree" end of the room, follows up on Annie's remark, "We shouldn't intervene unless it affects us."

"We wouldn't have any allies if we didn't," responds Tommy, a White boy standing even further toward the "disagree" end of the spectrum.

"What allies do we have now?" queries Danny, an African American boy who has placed himself closer towards the "agree" side of the room. "Don't we have only Britain? Don't we have like no allies?"

"It depends. Don't we want to help people from being abused?" asks Mary, a White girl standing closer to the "disagree" poster.

"If it's none of our business, everyone thinks we're the bad guys," Annie chimes in again. "Don't we have enough problems of our own? Then they'd just hate us more."

"You know when things are happening in other countries that are just morally wrong? You would just stand aside? Like a huge act of genocide?" challenges Cindy, a White girl standing quite close to the "disagree" side.

"Yeah. But what do we have the U.N. for?" asks Tariq, whose Uzbeki family had immigrated to the United States from Afghanistan.

"It's happening right now," offers a student.

"It's risky," adds Seema, an Indian American student.

"The United States is a huge world power. We need to take responsibility around the world," argues Rebecca, a White student.

"That's what the U.N. is for."

"It's not a military force," Rebecca responds.

"They solve world problems and stuff," counters Annie.

"We see people are crying out and we have to help them because we have power," says Rebecca. Murmurs fill the room.

"If they want to kill an entire race that makes no sense," Annie says forcefully. "That's just wrong. But sometimes it's none of our business."

"It's like somebody going into your house and telling you how to raise your family," explains Tariq.

In this segment of a longer discussion, students engaged with one another over a complex, weighty question. Notice the balance of teacher and student talk. Unlike most classroom discussions, which are dominated by individual exchanges between students and teacher, with the teacher both initiating and commenting on every student statement, in this slice of classroom talk we hear only two teacher statements. The first is organizational ("We're going to play Take-a-Stand"), and the second lays out the topic for the day ("The United States should not intervene in foreign countries"). After these two teacher offerings, the students speak back and forth among each other 17 times, with 10 individuals participating and without teacher prodding, correction, opining, or intervention.

Students voice their own opinions ("I'm on the fence because it depends on circumstances"; "We shouldn't intervene unless it affects us"; "We need to take responsibility around the world"). They pose questions for the group ("What allies do we have now?"; "Don't we want to help people from being abused?"; "But what do we have the U.N. for?"). They engage with these student-posed questions ("It's not a military force") and build upon one another's comments. They seem unafraid to disagree ("They solve world problems and stuff") and use metaphors to argue their perspectives ("It's like somebody going into your house and telling you how to raise your family").

In this classroom, then, students are engaging in authentic discussion of an essential civic question, puzzling through long-standing and unresolved civic issues that affect them directly. When should the United States intervene in the affairs of other countries?; What do we owe our allies?; What of the moral issue of people suffering under their own leaders?; Does greater responsibility come with greater power? The students do not resolve these issues. Nor should they. These 15 and 16 year olds, from backgrounds as diverse as the nation itself, are becoming participants in the ongoing debates and dilemmas of civic life. Moreover, the social studies classroom itself has been transformed from a space of boredom, repetition, and coverage of, as Janet put it earlier, "what has happened already," into a vibrant setting in which young people's interactions with each other unfold in surprising and interesting ways, like discussion in other parts of our lives.

A Closer Look at the Civic Benefits of Discussion

Social studies educators and others concerned with youth civic engagement have long argued that classroom discussions are an essential component of effective civic education (Hess, 2004, 2009). Larson and Parker assert that discussion is "arguably the centerpiece of democratic education because it engages students in *the* essential practice of democratic living" (1996, p. 110). In 2003 The Civic Mission of Schools report endorsed discussion as a key "promising approach" for civic education, recommending that educators "Incorporate discussion of current, local, national, and international issues and events in the classroom, particularly those that young people view as important" (p. 6).[1]

What makes discussion so essential to students' education for citizenship? Classroom discussion helps students dialogue across difference, learn about diverse perspectives, and consider opposing viewpoints. It is a good way to build students' critical thinking, and speaking and listening skills. Discussion can raise students' interest in civic issues, increase learning and content, and help to forge connections between students' lives and the material.

In a diverse democracy, the ability to listen and communicate across differences of all sorts is essential (Hess, 2004). Students at the three study schools valued the exchange of ideas in discussion. They valued and had a genuine interest in the varied opinions of their peers. "[E]veryone has something valid to say and something valuable to contribute," said Rebecca. "I like to think that I'm right all the time, but I'm not right all the time." Robbie felt that "personally I like talking to people and telling my opinion . . . it was just really cool seeing what other people thought about the same things." Vinne concurred, saying "It was really good to hear everybody's arguments and why people think so strongly about a subject, and the reasoning behind the facts." Antonio enthused:

> the class has been really inspiration . . . I really do like it because the class is always open to discussion. We hear other people's opinions . . . It's really a

---

1 Written and endorsed by 50 leading scholars and practitioners at meetings orchestrated by the Center for Information and Research on Civic Learning and Engagement, and the Carnegie Corporation.

great class because you hear other people's opinions . . . it makes the class just easier and more enjoyable to be at.

Students sometimes changed their own opinions as a result of discussion. Manuel shared that "most of the times in class changed my opinion, changed my point of view looking at stuff." Robbie explained that:

> we had someone did one side of the issue and right after that someone on the other side of the issue. And before that I was for it, and now I'm against it . . . because of what the people said, so the research that somebody did, and just having somebody explain it to me like that, it changed my mind.

Samara gave an example of a discussion that changed her mind about an issue:

> illegal immigration. Like, before I thought it was okay because some people couldn't come in because of certain reasons. But then after a while I was like, it does affect us a lot, the people that are already here, and there's people waiting in line doing it the legal way.

Rebecca shared, "And I've definitely seen a lot of my classmates switch sides, and then switch back again."

Students appreciated that differing opinions were part of diversity and that talking through difference was a learned skill. Rebecca described:

> "I think there should be a war." "I think there shouldn't be a war." That it's just an opinion. At the end of the day we all are just human and you and still be civil or even friends with someone and have a different opinion from them and debate with them. And disagree.

Discussion promotes higher order thinking skills (Chilcoat & Ligon, 2001; Hess, 2004; Larson, 1999; Passe & Evans, 1996). Oral expression and listening skills are strengthened through their use in the classroom. Jill Tenney saw this in her students' use of discussion, describing their progress in "discussion skills, listening skills, public speaking, feeling comfortable voicing their opinions. Being OK to maybe have an alternative viewpoint than someone else and being able to discuss it." Rebecca reflected that "at the beginning of the year we would talk over each other and interrupt all the time. But I think we learned the value of just hearing someone else out."

Discussion raises students' interest in civic issues. Andolina et al. (2003) found that students' interest levels rose significantly when they reported being encouraged to have open discussion. Narciso said "we'd be talking about work, doing our work, you know, about history. We'd be like, where's the guns made at? What's causing this?" Samara said the discussion that stuck in her mind the most was "about the Palestinian and the Israel war. Because it was something that we all got really into and we debated a lot over it . . . everybody was getting so involved." Henry in Oak Knoll explained, "everybody participates in class because we talk about topics that relate to everybody, not just one person . . . like segregation, everybody has something to say about that."

Through discussion, students connected the civic to the personal. Vinnie reflected on a particularly interesting discussion. "Immigration," he said, "we had a class discussion on immigration. I have two parents that are immigrants, you know. It's something that . . . it's personal, it's personal. And you know, just hearing out the arguments, just understanding what my parents went through."

Discussion can contribute to deeper understanding of social studies content (Hess, 2004). Through discussion, teachers can monitor student understanding of content knowledge (Okolo, Ferreti, & MacArthur, 2007). Students felt they learned and retained more through discussion. Said Peter from Oak Knoll, "I'd rather be able to speak our minds than just be lectured all day. I think it's much more fun . . . We had discussions and after a while it sticks in your mind more." Samara from Allwood echoed this idea, telling us that "most students study better that way, like learn better." As Narciso described,

> if we have a discussion, people actually got to learn about it more. Like we'll know a little bit about it, and that's not right. So like, the next day we'll focus on that one topic that we was talking about so we'll know a lot about it. And we won't say the wrong stuff and we'll know what we're talking about.

Students also noticed factual errors and clarified misunderstandings of content during discussion. Robbie from Allwood described a discussion in which a student portraying Hillary Clinton's perspective put forward contradictory opinions, saying "Hillary Clinton had like two opinions. So somebody didn't do their research right." Robbie explained,

> that was a good chance to ask questions too, if you didn't understand something . . . you could ask it as part of the seminar . . . to ask your classmates. So it definitely opened up communication about what we learned. And sometimes you'd find out, like if you missed something, and someone else says it . . . You learn more from that, from than just what you learned in the lesson.

Students appreciated the opportunity to surface their own and their classmates' misunderstandings through discussion, learning from one another, not only from the teacher.

Similarly, Allwood teacher Jill Tenney described how she saw her students' content knowledge was deepened and clarified through discussion:

> They all understand what's going on, they all have a viewpoint and they all have an opinion. It may not be correct and there may be some things that are false, but through discussion the kids will point it out to each other.

She provided a specific example of how discussion led to clarification of student misunderstanding, the case of students mixing up responsibility for the September 11, 2001 terrorist attacks.

> When we had a discussion about Iraq and Afghanistan, a few kids messed up, or we were talking about 9/11, a few kids misinterpreted who was responsible for that. Was it, you know, the Taliban and Osama bin Laden, or was it Saddam Hussein. And a few kids pointed it out to each other. And they said "no, you're wrong, you're talking about the wrong war." And through discussion, those misunderstandings that those kids had came to light and the realized "OK, I'm not correct."

She noted that, without discussion, such misunderstandings would never even see the light of day:

> without discussion that kid sits in that classroom and leaves that classroom not understanding fully what's the difference between Osama bin Laden and Saddam Hussein. Because they were never able to say or to verbally express that they were wrong . . . And no one would be able to correct them. So I think that the discussion was the most valuable part of class.

Discussion was, for Ms. Tenney, a way to reach deep into students' thinking about key historical events while foregrounding active student exploration of ideas and events, avoiding teacher-focused instruction blind to student knowledge or interest.

Through discussion in the classroom, students were able to experience an authentic exchange of ideas that went beyond stale recitations and mirrored the vibrant talk we long to have outside of the classroom. Kristi at Allwood described the Socratic seminars in her class:

> the whole class [would sit in a big circle], and then we would take turns and most of the time we wouldn't even raise our hands . . . She didn't want us to sit there and be like "OK, can I go," because then that's not how it is. In real life you're not going to sit there, raise your hand to talk to someone . . . it was kind of like experiencing how life is itself like besides history.

Framed by the themes and questions described in Chapter 2, discussion facilitated students making two sorts of connections—the connection between the issue under study and current events, and the connection between the issue under study and their own lives.

Moreover, over the course of the year teachers saw their students' discussion skills develop. As Ms. Tenney described,

> I mean, at the beginning of the year, I'll use period one as an example, period one was silent. We would do Socratic seminar and they wouldn't say a word, and you know, it was really like pulling teeth. And towards the end of the year, they you know were completely fine talking to one another, they were completely fine discussing different viewpoints with one another and a lot of times, especially in that class, we had situations where we did Take-a-Stand , and there would be one person on the other side, or two people on the other side, arguing certain viewpoints. And they felt totally comfortable doing it, and I think that the last presentation that they did on Social Protests, we really saw some of the students who would never be comfortable standing up in front of the room in the beginning of the year, openly talk about their social protest, take questions, volunteer their own opinions, relate it to essential questions, and that was not happening, that would have never happened in September or October.

Discussion was thus both an essential pedagogy for civic learning and a key civic skill for students to master.

Is Discussion Taking Place in Most Social Studies Classrooms?

Sadly, despite the strong research justification for integrating discussion into the classroom for civic benefit, lively and authentic discussion on key civic themes does not often occur in social studies classrooms, and, indeed, is all too rare within school classrooms in general. Multiple studies report that little discussion occurs in social studies classrooms; even teachers who claim to use discussion are often confusing it with question and answer and recitation (Chilcoat & Ligon, 2001; Hahn, 1996; Hess & Posselt, 2002; Nystrand, Gamoran, & Carbonaro, 1998; Wilen, 2003). Wolk writes that "Not allowing students to engage in open discussion on important issues and topics is the most detrimental intellectual void in schools" (2003, p. 103).

Students at the three study schools confirmed this assertion. Reflecting on their previous year's social studies class, Surrey student Sarah explained "[last year we would] just answer the questions." Allwood student Rebecca described the closest practice to discussion in her previous year's social studies class, "It was usually the teacher would stand in the front and just . . . I mean it wasn't really an organized class discussion." "So we really didn't have discussions then," Tariq from Allwood explained, "it was more like the teacher, you know, it was the teacher teaching and us taking notes." "I'm used to history classes where it's just book work, book work, book work," reflected Allwood's Antonio. Peter, who had transferred to Oak Knoll from a school in a different city, reflected "my other school is just lectures, lectures, lectures, and it gets boring after a while so you don't really remember."

Lack of discussion seemed to characterize students' schools. "We basically never do that [discussion] in none of my classes except Mr. Brooks'," Narciso explained. "Mr. Brooks' class is like one of the best classes I have because he actually sits there and listens . . ." Our early survey confirmed these reflections. 56% of Surrey students, 63% of Allwood students and 48% of Oak Knoll students responded that in their last year's social studies classes they worked mostly from a textbook, and 78%, 51%, and 50% of Surrey, Allwood, and Oak Knoll students surveyed described these previous classes as places where "teachers mainly lectured and students took notes." As noted earlier, much of what teachers call discussion is actually teacher-directed question and answer, recitation designed to elicit specific student response and move the class through coverage of particular material.

With all the benefits described earlier, what prevents teachers from leading open discussions in their classrooms? Teachers do not attempt to lead discussion for a variety of reasons, some easily addressed, others more fundamental and requiring substantive shifts in how they and their schools conceptualize learning.

Many teachers are wary of discussion, concerned that it takes valuable classroom time (Dillon, 1994; Larson, 1999). Bob Banks had this same concern. During an early interview he expressed concerns about timing, saying "all I know is I'm not going to be able to implement as much as we were planning on. It's not going to be possible. Because doing one structured conversation has taken three days." Bob voiced concerns about "the curricular value" of discussions that were framed around student exploration of the connections between their own experiences and the issue under study, and was concerned about spending time on an activity not specifically designed to cover particular material.

Wilen (2003) notes that many teachers believe the purpose of education is the transmission of fixed knowledge from teacher to student. Discussion, if it is to have the benefits previously described, upsets this notion, requiring the teacher to give up authority and for questions to be raised (and answered) by students. Proceeding rapidly through a content-laden curriculum, particularly with a chronological structure that encourages a coverage orientation, is at odds with the unpredictable, exploratory nature of authentic and connective discussion. Discussion does not move students predictably through a predetermined set of material. Indeed, if it does it risks losing the organic, relational quality that students prize, that we prize in good discussions.

Authentic discussion requires teachers to give up authority in a system that is based on authority, and promote exploration and expression in settings in which learning is seen as quantifiable and measurable, and this can be a difficult shift for teachers with a different orientation toward knowledge.

Some teachers may feel that their students are not capable of discussion. Dillon (1994) speculates that our lofty ideas about discussion and language for describing it make it seem like an advanced activity only suitable for some students. Bob Banks reflected, when explaining why he did not conduct as many discussions as he had originally planned, "I didn't think that these regular level kids would be able to hack a Socratic seminar or the structure of a Take-a-Stand or the structure of a structured conversation." He was uncomfortable with formats that were more open-ended, saying "Seminar, the way I understood it, it was too freeform." He saw a tension between his sense of his students' abilities and the possibility of discussion in his classroom. "They're regular level kids," he explained, "They need processing time."

Such preconceptions about discussion can be confirmed when teachers are ill-prepared to structure and effectively lead discussions in their classrooms (Chilcoat & Ligon, 2001; Dillon, 1994). They may talk too much, or ask inauthentic or ineffective questions (Hess, 2004; Wilen, 2003). Students, for their part, may be unprepared to contribute well or may contribute unevenly (Hess, 2004). Kevin commented that at times discussion floundered in his classroom due to students' lack of knowledge or interest. Bob was concerned about uneven participation by students and his ability to pick "the right" topic, saying,

> It is just a matter of how do I pick what's essential, you know. How do I, how do I choose what's essential. If I'm opening it up to genuine student interest and dialogue, then if I pick a real clunker than it's a waste of forty minutes.

These are critical issues that must be addressed for open classroom discussion to successfully take place.

Three Approaches to Talking Civics

After reading and discussing research on the efficacy of discussion for civic learning, the project team agreed upon the importance of discussion as a key civic skill strand, both a pedagogy for connecting students' experiences with the issues and questions under study and a civic skill worth cultivating. The team agreed that after a year of participating in the discussion strand of the problem-posing curriculum, students should be able to do the following:

- consider and discuss key issues and controversies in civic life
- argue a point in a coherent way, using evidence
- back up opinion with fact
- make/see connections between topics
- listen actively to others' arguments, to understand and engage
- connect their own lives and concerns to civic issues and the curriculum.

To do this, we selected three forms of discussion that would repeat over the course of the year, giving students an opportunity to become comfortable with each format: Socratic seminar, Take-a-Stand, and structured conversation.

Each discussion form addressed different aspects of the goals. The repetition of the three formats allowed for students to develop comfort and skill with each approach, the variety mitigated tedium. Jill Tenney reflected that,

> I think the repetition of the same type of activities, but, like with Take-a-Stand, repetitive, at least once a marking period, allowed them to achieve a comfort level where they knew the activity they knew the rules of the activity they knew when people could speak, when people couldn't speak. Because of the repetition, it allowed for the building. Whereas in years past, yeah we used discussion, we used debate, and I used different activities in the classroom, it wasn't focused around the same types of skills . . . one marking period we'd have a debate and the next marking period maybe we'd do something different. But I think because you're using the same kind of technique, they become comfortable with it, they know it, and then they can build on it.

I will describe and give examples of each form below.

Socratic seminar. A Socratic seminar is a student-centered discussion, often based on a text, designed to enlarge students' understandings on a topic or text. In a Socratic seminar students sit so they can see each other, usually in a circle. The teacher uses open-ended questions to initiate the seminar, keeps notes on student comments, and occasionally interjects to summarize themes in the discussion and pose questions designed to move students into fruitful territory. Students participate freely in the discussion, using visual cues and self-monitoring rather than hand-raising to take turns. As Kristi from Allwood put it, "we would take turns and like we would most of the time we wouldn't even raise our hands."

Socratic seminars allow students to pursue issues and ideas in an open-ended forum, to look each other in the eye, to slow the pace and think deeply about how the themes and questions connected to their own lives. Tredway (1995) writes that,

> the first axiom of involving students actively in the learning process is to relate activities to their own experiences, thereby engaging them on an emotional level . . . A potent learning model that does just this is the Socratic seminar, a form of structured discourse about ideas and moral dilemmas.
>
> *(p. 26)*

Perhaps the most familiar of the three discussion formats, Parker and Hess (2001, p. 282) describe seminars as "discussion aimed at developing, exposing, and exploring meanings." An example will illustrate this idea.

In Kevin's special needs U.S. History II class, seven students (five African American and two Latino) participated in a Socratic seminar to kick off the Conflict and Resolution theme. The seminar fragment described below shows how seminars can be used to bridge the gap between students' own concerns and essential civic issues.

Mr. Brooks begins the seminar by reading aloud a quote, commonly thought to have been penned by 18th-century Irish statesman and political theorist Edmund Burke: "The only thing necessary for the triumph of evil is for good men to do nothing."

"What do you think Gustavo?" Mr. Brooks asks a Latino boy. "Is Edmund Burke full of crap? Was there ever a time when you saw something wrong and you did nothing?"

Gustavo doesn't reply. A second student walks into the classroom, Elliot. Mr. Brooks welcomes him to class and involves him in the seminar.

"Elliot, look at the quote. What do you think?"

"Oh yeah, yeah," Elliot responds, reading the quote from the board. "Because if they do nothing, it's just going to grow. I don't think anyone is good."

"What about you Gustavo?" Mr. Brooks asks, probing the reluctant student. "Are you a good person?"

"No," Gustavo responds.

"Was there ever a time when you didn't do anything about a problem in your community?" asks Mr. Brooks.

"I was picking up my nephew," offers Elliot, "and some dudes were fighting and people called the cops and no one said anything. No one gave cops info about the fight."

"If I asked you that," Mr. Brooks persists, "what do you think it [the quote] means? For evil to happen, good people must sit back and do nothing."

"It's true," says Miguel loudly, with feeling. "Yes, there's a lot in this community that you see that you can't do something about—drugs."

"Suppose you thought something was right—is it always right to get involved?" pressed Mr. Brooks.

"You know drugs are bad but you can't fix it," responds Elliot.

"What about drug dealers," asks Mr. Brooks, bringing in a common local example, "you see them in the same spot, same day, all the time."

Elliot shifts responsibility for doing something about drug dealers to law enforcement, saying "If they [cops] came everyday, they'd move because they won't make money."

"What if you were to report them?" asks Mr. Brooks, not letting the class off the hook for their participation in this community problem.

"You can't snitch in the hood," proclaims Manuel. "You get popped."

For a few minutes the students discuss whether or not one person can make a difference, then Mr. Brooks segues into the broader issue at hand, the essential question for the Conflict and Resolution theme.

"Should our country get involved in other countries' business?" he asks.

"NO!" exclaim all of the students in the class.

"We're at war now *because* of that," Sandra says [emphasis added].

"They trying to come here and kill us because we're over there killing people," adds Elliot.

In this seminar segment, Mr. Brooks begins with a quotation for the students to consider, one which could be equally applicable to the students' own lives, events in history, and current happenings. He takes care to pull students into the discussion, directly questioning them, regardless of whether they came late to class or not. He pushes on students, probing them to explain their views and challenging them to think about the other side of their perspective. He connects the issue at hand directly to students' own experiences, and doesn't shy away from challenging questions ("What about you, are you a good person?"; "What if you were to report them?").

In this discussion, students' in Kevin's classroom grappled with a complex statement related to the theme of Conflict and Resolution and the essential question of "Why does the U.S. go to war?". Interpreting Burke's statement through the context of their daily lives in beleaguered Surrey, students described the impediments they felt they would face if they tried to "make a difference" in their own community. This sense of needing to mind one's own business, the futility or even danger or intervention, was echoed by the students' belief that the United States should stay out of the affairs of other countries.

Throughout the course of the project, seminars made it possible for students to make connections between their own lives, current issues, and enduring civic themes. Ms. Tenney described how a Socratic seminar on child labor during the Economics theme allowed her students, many of whom were recent immigrants, to connect their study of the industrialization with current issues and personal experiences. "The discussion that we had in class is something that you normally don't see," she said, "because not only were they relating child labor in the United States and child labor around the world, and they were looking at it from both viewpoints and why it's a catch 22, but also bringing their own experiences into it, because we have such a diverse community that they've actually experienced, maybe not they themselves, but through the countries that they came from, some form of child labor."

Take-a-Stand. A Take-a-Stand discussion is a "discussion-in-motion." During a Take-a-Stand, students array themselves physically in response to a statement or set of statements posed by the teacher. The teacher posts the word "agree" on one side of the room and the word "disagree" on the other side (or "yes" and "no," depending upon the phrasing of the statements). The teacher then makes a statement, and students choose where to stand, according to their opinion on the statement. The teacher facilitates a discussion (while students are standing) in which students speak about why they are standing in a particular place, posing questions to students standing in other spots. Students can move if they change their opinions, and can be asked to explain the reason behind their move. In some classrooms, students become so adept at the practice that they require little to no adult facilitation after the initial statement is made.

Take-a-Stand discussions shake up the physical space of the classroom, allowing students to use their bodies to position and reposition themselves on an issue, adding a playful and kinesthetic aspect to class. Teachers are forced to think carefully to craft provocative statements on which students can take varied stances, and then stay out of the ensuing discourse. Some of the liveliest, most intense, and engaged classroom discussions occurred in this format, particularly in Jill Tenney's classroom.

Students valued the way the format both showcased different viewpoints and allowed for them to change their minds, and to physically indicate that change to others. Jennie described how,

> Whenever we would be taking a stand and I would be on the fence, usually my mind would change. So well that helps because I don't like the things where I'm not sure of. I like being one way or another so. That would help. Sometimes I switched sides completely.

Victor thought it was

> always cool to see how the class was divided up, from one side, to being on the fence, to being on the other side. It was really good to hear everybody's arguments and you know, why people think so strongly about a subject, and you know, the reasoning behind the facts.

Samara also liked the format, saying, "Well this year was more interesting cause we got to switch sides all the time. Last year, like we had to pick one side and if we thought it was different, we couldn't change it." Students were deeply interested in each other's opinions, and appreciative of the way the format allowed them to listen, consider, and change their minds over the course of the discussion.

A fragment from a Take-a-Stand on Afghanistan that occurred in Ms. Tenney's classroom two years after the initial study demonstrates some of the mechanics and advantages of the format. In this lesson, students had been studying about U.S. military presence in Afghanistan, taking three different, assigned perspectives on the issue: launch a counterinsurgency against the Taliban in Afghanistan; use counterterrorism in Afghanistan and Pakistan to fight Al Qaeda, not the Taliban; or support a regional approach to the problem of Afghanistan and withdraw our troops.

After about 25 minutes of interaction, with students representing assigned perspectives based on reading they had done the night before, Ms. Tenney segued seamlessly a Take-a-Stand on the issue.

"Yield!" says Ms. Tenney loudly. "President Obama was correct in sending 30,000 more troops to Afghanistan. That side," she points to the right-hand side of the room, "is 'YES,' the other side," she points to the opposite side of the room, "is 'NO.'"

The words "YES" and "NO" are written on opposite sides of the whiteboard at the front of the room.

"Those in the middle," she continues, "you have four comments and then you have to choose a side."

Without hesitation all 20 of the students in the room stand up and move to different positions. Ten are standing by the YES side, six by the NO side and four are in the middle. They begin to discuss.

"I agree he did the right thing," says a student standing on the YES side of the room. "He's thinking more about our security than about his popularity."

"Why?" responds a NO student. "Why did he have to send more over there?; Why not leave the same amount?"

The discussion continues, with many different students speaking. Throughout the discussion students shift sides as their opinions change, and the students sitting in the middle move to one side or the other. After several minutes the teacher changes the statement.

"Yield!" says Ms. Tenney. "Terrorism is the biggest threat to our national security."

The students reshuffle, moving to the different sides of the room, ten standing by the YES side, four by the NO side, and six in the middle.

"What else is a possible threat?" queries a student standing on the YES side.

"There are lots of countries that don't like us and have the capacity of building nuclear weapons," responds a student from the NO side. "That's more of a threat than terrorism."

The conversation continues for several minutes. Eventually there are eight students on the NO side and 12 on the YES side. The teacher changes the statement again.

"Yield!" proclaims Ms. Tenney, "Pakistan is our ally."

The students again move around the room, taking stands on this statement. Two students are by the YES side, twelve stand by NO, and six are in the middle.

"If they were our ally wouldn't they let us come in and search for Al Qaeda?" ask a student from the NO side.

"Name one of our closest allies" a YES-side student queries. Someone shouts "Britain." "OK, would Britain just let us come in and search for Al Qaeda?"

The discussion continues, again with many students speaking and students moving sides throughout. Marissa, a student from a Pakistani family, has the final comment, saying "I think terrorists are ruining lives in Pakistan, killing innocent people. People I even know, they died because of terrorist bombing there."

This Take-a-Stand reveals the familiarity students had developed with the format and the underlying rules adopted by the class. Students moved immediately into position when the teacher made the first statement, and shifted without prompting during the discussion. By the fourth comment, all students knew they must take a side and did so. They responded to each other rather than to the teacher, asked each other questions, built upon each other's responses, and disagreed respectfully with one another's positions. The students brought forward evidence and examples to argue their points, and listened carefully to one another.

This structure allowed the class to maximize the time spent engaging in meaningful discussion. The flexibility of movement allowed students to express themselves without feeling backed into a corner; indeed, there was an expectation that students would shift position throughout the activity. The act of standing breaks through the assumption that learning in school only takes place from a seated position, perhaps addressing the physical restlessness that can result from this passive positioning.

Structured conversation. A structured conversation is a small group discussion based on written material presenting different perspectives on an issue. During a structured conversation, students work in pairs to read and identify the main points of one side of a controversial issue. Each pair is then matched up with another pair that has read and prepared to discuss the opposite side of the issue. Pairs take turns sharing information, eventually dropping their assigned position to discuss the issue, trying to either reach agreement, or clarify their points of disagreement.

Structured conversation, experienced by students as the most school-like and arduous of the discussion formats, forced students to consider both sides of an issue, to read carefully and articulate positions thoroughly, to use evidence from text, and to discuss from outside of their own opinion.

In the following example, students in Ms. Tenney's class took part in a structured conversation on war economies. The class was divided into groups of four or five. The group in this example has five students (three are on one side), two South Asian American girls, one South Asian American boy, one East Asian American boy, and a White girl. When I sat down with them, the students were in the midst of writing down points from the articles they read comparing the costs of the wars in Iraq and Vietnam.

"Cost of Iraq war and also the Vietnam war," said the boy, explaining to his group, which is trying to show how the Vietnam War was much more expensive than the war in Iraq.

"What else?" his partner asks.

"This is what I highlighted," the boy responds.

"How much we spent on each and which one was more expensive. Vietnam was a billion a month. I'm not sure which are the main points."

Ms. Tenney kneels next to the group. "Remember yesterday we talked about your paragraph writing and not using facts to back up the statement? Don't just generalize."

A student from the opposing side checks on the progress of the other pair, saying "You guys have your three main points?"

"Yeah."

"Your turn," a boy says to his partner.

"Our reading is about casualty of war on the U.S. economy," says the girl. "The war is costing too much. It already costed 3.14 billion dollars already."

"Billion?" asks her partner.

"Billion," she responds.

"50,000 casualties," the boy adds.

"Bracket that together and write the cost *quote* 'in money and blood' because that's how they summarize it," says the girl.

A girl from the opposing side asks "What's your third point."

"It's not like well thought out."

"Not thought out?"

"That's why it's costing money and blood. Next pair."

The girl on the other side begins, saying to her partner "I'll read the first one, you do the second one. The war in Iraq is costing 5 billion per month, while war in Vietnam costed 9 billion per month."

"Second one," her partner, a boy, continues. "150,000 troops sent to Iraq while 500,000 troops sent to Vietnam. And what does this mean? Bigger budget."

"After Vietnam," the girl responds.

Ms. Tenney comes back to the group, listening in.

"U.S. economies during wars are similar," begins the girl, "because . . ."

". . . billions are being spent," concludes her partner.

"U.S. economies during wars are different," summarizes another girl, "because . . . similar because thousands of troops are being spent, troops are being killed. Are different because . . ."

"Different amounts spent," says a girl, writing. "Different . . ." trailing off.

"Can we go back to similarities?" asks Ms. Tenney. "Costing a lot of money. And what does that do to the economy?"

"See," one of the boys says to his partner, "I said we were talking about the economy."

The structured conversation does not have the same authentic quality as the previous two discussion formats. Rather than delving into their own opinions, students grappled with complex readings and worked to nail down the different perspectives on an issue. They then needed to articulate those perspectives for other students, and summarize the two sides. This proved to be a useful way for students to engage with difficult concepts and fully understand different perspectives on complex issues.

Five Steps to Structure Authentic Discussions that Promote Civic Learning

From this research, I would like to offer five key principles for teaching with discussion for civic learning: create a safe and open setting, offer an underlying structure, train students to use that structure, have something interesting for them to discuss, and then step back and get (mostly) out of the way.

Create an Open and Safe Setting

A safe, open classroom atmosphere is essential to discussion (Hess & Posselt, 2002). Classrooms must be places where all opinions are reflected (Evans & Saxe, 1996), free from fear of personal attacks (Cook & Tashlik, 2004), encouraging, in which the teacher is not critical or judgmental (Hess, 2004) and does not encourage tension or combativeness (Passe & Evans, 1996).

Students in the three study schools reflected the importance of the classroom as a safe space for discussion. As Vinnie from Allwood described, for good discussion, participants needed to "have respect for what other people say and not like badgering people, you know, bad mouthing them." The safe, open atmosphere gave the classroom a more intimate feel, according to Tariq. In Ms. Tenney's classroom, "it was so much like open discussion that you thought you were just hanging out with a bunch of friends."

Discussion also facilitated a deeper connection between students and their teacher. Manuel from Surrey explained that,

> Mr. Brooks' class is like one of the best classes I have because, like, he actually sits there and listens to me . . . And he tells you, like, sometimes we're right, and he's like "oh yeah you right," and sometimes we're wrong and he corrects you. And that's what we need, communication. And some kids too, like, they don't have people to talk to, they got a lot problems in their family and don't have nobody to talk to. Mr. Brooks, you know what

I'm saying, like at the beginning of the year, he opened that type of relationship with his kids, that he can talk to, they can talk to him.

Discussion, after all, is a human interaction, with the potential to deepen connections and need for kindness and understanding.

Offer an Underlying Structure

Researchers agree that good classroom discussions need an underlying structure to prevent discussion failure through either lack of engagement or chaos (Cook & Tashlik, 2004; Passe & Evans, 1996). Discussion can and should be structured in ways that give all students a chance to participate, encourage students to speak to one another and not just to the teacher, encourage listening, allow students to change their minds, and help students identify disagreement and ask questions about those disagreements (Passe & Evans, 1996; Singleton & Giese, 1996). A variety of structures, accompanied by basic rules, can facilitate these qualities (Passe & Evans, 1996); this chapter explored three.

Train Students in That Structure

Inexperienced students must be prepared to discuss (Cook & Tashlik, 2004). Students need adequate background knowledge (Hess, 2004; Passe & Evans, 1996) and must be taught to use evidence (Cook & Tashlik, 2004). Students can be taught how to recognize roadblocks in discussion and reflect on the quality of the discussion (Singleton & Giese, 1996). As Jill Tenney described,

> before we did a Socratic seminar we'd actually have to talk about how you talk to people, what you say, when it's appropriate, and kind of go through that behavior of maybe a simulated Socratic seminar, how we're supposed to act before we went into the actual discussion and like let them go ... with the Take-a-Stand activity, we talk about how to move from one side of the room to the other.

To train students to participate in Socratic seminars, Ms. Tenney first conducted one seminar to get them comfortable, then, for the second seminar, she gave them points for how many times they spoke, gradually moving to a consideration of specific qualities of their points (i.e. use of evidence, clarity).

By the middle of the first semester in Ms. Tenney's classroom, students moved quickly into position for the various forms of discussion without elaborate instruction. An example of this is the discussion segment I presented earlier in this chapter, in which the teacher's statement "We're going to play Take-a-Stand" was all that was needed for students to array themselves in the room according to their initial stance on an issue. When students receive training and adequate content preparation they can enter discussion on an equal footing, ready to participate.

Have Something Interesting to Discuss and Use Real Questions

Just as Chapter 2 described how questions and topics are important to a meaningful curriculum, so are they critical to effective discussion. Topics have to be interesting to the students (Passe & Evans, 1996; Singleton & Giese, 1996). As Manuel from Surrey put it, a good discussion was "When it actually grabs my attention." Questions need to be authentic and open-ended, without a correct answer (Chilcoat & Ligon, 2001; Hahn, 1996; Hess, 2004; Passe & Evans, 1996). Questions can be employed to push students to think critically and further their ideas and arguments (Cook & Tashlik, 2004; Passe & Evans, 1996). During discussion, students' questions to the teacher can be redirected toward their peers to encourage authentic conversation; students should be encouraged to ask questions as well (Hahn, 1996; Whitehouse, 2008; Wilen, 2001). In this project, the thematic organization and essential questions greatly facilitated the generation of interesting, meaningful questions, and topics for discussion.

Step Back and Get (Mostly) Out of the Way: "She Just Let Us Talk"

Once the stage is set for discussion, the challenge for the teacher is to figure out how to step back and get out of the way. This can be the most difficult task for teachers, who are, after all, professionals whose work so often involves commanding center stage. It is, however, arguably the most essential part of enabling authentic, open discussion.

Part of the teacher's role is to get discussion started. Ms. Tenney's students described her as a "moderator" and a "conversation starter." "She's just the, you know, she's the moderator," explained Rebecca. "She tried to stay out of it because I think if a teacher becomes too over, you know just kind of like breathing down your necks and trying to force their opinion I mean that's not what education's about." Robbie echoed Rebecca's language, saying "She um, basically she's the moderator. She'll throw out a question, and then whoever wants to start, starts." Tariq used a metaphor to describe Ms. Tenney's role of "conversation starter." "You ever go to like a party and the party motivators? That's what she pretty much was." The teacher's role, then, was understood by the students to be getting the discussion started; their role was to actually discuss.

Once discussion was started, the teacher's key task was to step back and get out of the way. "She gave us the topic and just let us talk," explained Jeannie. This involved foregrounding the students' talk and opinions and declining to offer her own. "She mostly stepped back," as Janet put it.

This was a tricky feat that Ms. Tenney made appear deceptively easy, but actually took a great deal of thought and forbearance. She had to carefully circumscribe her own reactions, particularly at the beginning of the year. She described the first seminar of the year, when, despite being seated in a circle and directed to speak to one another, the students repeatedly addressed her,

> the first seminar that we had, every time they were speaking about an issue or where they stood, it was directed at me . . . And I was kind of, I had my head down, because if I make eye contact . . .

By sitting outside the circle during seminars or in the back of the room during other discussion formats and not making eye contact, Ms. Tenney gradually trained the students to speak to and engage with one another rather than with her. "I kind of tried to ignore them a little bit," she said, "and they kind of went on their own."

This was a retraining process, in which students needed to be weaned away from the need for constant teacher reassurance and dependence on the teacher for all information.

> They're so used to, you know for so many years, that you are the source of information. And that they need approval from you, that's, that's the one thing that I'm not going to give them is that when they make a comment I'm not going to give them that approval that they're always looking for. Because they'll, they'll make a comment in the form of a question. Because they want you to say "oh yes, you're right."

Ms. Tenney found that if she responded to student queries during discussion, she then became the focal point around which all student talk revolved. She therefore needed to refrain from any comment that was not aimed at moving the discussion along.

This could be particularly difficult when students offered incorrect information to each other. Ms. Tenney felt it was worthwhile to hold back during these moments as well, and allow students to eventually correct one another.

> That's always a tough line to walk. I think that if it's inaccurate, I'd rather the students point it out than for me to point it out. I think it's my role to facilitate. In life people are wrong, they misjudge things, they don't understand things and I think that one of the skills is to point it out to your peers, that, no, you're just not right on that, and I would rather the kids do it than for me to do it.

Later, during the debriefing following the discussion, she could then make clarifications.

> When we debrief after Take-a-Stand, or after Socratic seminar, it will come to light that certain facts are right and certain facts are wrong, it may not be

that day, but it hopefully will be by the end of the unit that they would understand that they were not right.

There were times when she might step in, however, to preserve the safety of the classroom.

> The only time that I would stop it or clarify is if a student asked, or if it were something that would hurt, a comment would hurt someone else, if it was biased or racist or something. Something that would have to, you know, I would have to say, "hey, wait, you're out of line."

Preserving a hospitable classroom climate while de-centering the classroom from teacher domination took a great amount of skill.

Another difficult but essential component of getting out of students' ways to allow for discussion was learning to wait during periods of silence. Allowing time for students to think (the often touted "wait time") was difficult, but essential. As Jill Tenney described, "You know, you can't just jump in. They have to think. Take time, you know, it takes time to think. And it's hard, it's really hard to learn that, and know when to do that in the classroom." Her advice for new teachers,

> just be patient. And when you're being patient, and you think you're patient, be more patient. Because, you know, you get to the point and you just want to answer the question or you just want to jump in even though they're not done posing the question, and answer it. And you have just got to have that pause, and the pauses are ok. But, you know, as a teacher who might understand, you know, the curriculum or content, you just want to jump in there sometimes and you just kind of got to let it be quiet. And then when you think it's quiet, let it be quiet some more.

For authentic discussion, teachers need to allow the conversation to move and flow naturally, moving along with the currents of students' interests, their questions to each other and their engagement with each other's perspectives. This means that discussions do not always move in straight paths or "cover" material in the most linear of ways, but rather "chain off," according to student interest and opinion. As Ryan described Socratic seminars,

> it was just really cool seeing what other people what other people thought about the same things you thought about. And like who agree and how a conversation would start, and sometimes an argument would start just by a simple question. And those things kind of chain off, like one person will say something, and it will touch on another topic, and another person will compare, and it will get into that.

To accommodate this more natural flow, teachers cannot fear student disagreement, and must resist the urge to step in and settle points of conflict. This was difficult, as Ms. Tenney described, "not stepping in, that's the hardest. Especially as a new teacher. You don't know the line between losing control and still having control. It's a hard line."

Teacher neutrality is also important to allowing student voice and opinion to remain front and center. As Tariq described,

> like she'd throw a topic up there and then she would pretty much keep her mouth shut and she wouldn't let anyone use her as a reference. You know what I'm saying? Because her opinion might be different from everyone else's so she was just like "here's a topic. Now you guys talk about it," and if no one would talk she'd put it in other words or ask a question about it to get the conversation started. But she would never be like "oh this is my opinion and that's my opinion." She would never say that and I thought that was really important because like if a teacher voices out their opinion, of course it's going to like change the minds of a lot of people. It's like "oh they're the teacher. They must know a lot."

Teacher neutrality was important for providing students with the space they needed to form and voice their own opinions. In a context in which teachers were presumed to be the ultimate authority, authentic discussion would be difficult should the teacher put her stance front and center.

The teacher did not always refrain from participating, however. Janet described how Ms. Tenney would play "devil's advocate" should the discussion veer too far to one side.

> If we ever went, if we all went to one side, Miss Tenney would play devil's advocate. And she is so good at it. It would just frustrate me. Because I was like "I know you don't agree with what you're saying but you're so good at it."

This was important when students lacked some essential information. Janet continued, "some people . . . they're going to make points and they don't have the whole background story so they are kind of like thinking about it with really no actual facts. She would then play devil's advocate in that way."

As Tariq and Tamika, quoted at the very beginning of this chapter, indicate, good discussions are engaging in immediate, exciting, and personally meaningful ways that distinguish the activity from other forms of classroom instruction. Yet, discussion is a misunderstood, poorly wielded, and underutilized strategy in many social studies classrooms. Creating open, authentic discussions that can facilitate meaningful civic learning necessitates a shift in teachers' conceptions of knowledge and of their role as instructor. It is not necessary to feel you know everything about a topic to lead a discussion; indeed, a speculative stance toward the content may advance discussion more (Cook & Tashlik, 2004; Dillon, 1994). Teachers need to appear deeply interested in students' ideas and be willing to put their own opinions, beliefs, and even some of their favorite chunks of content in the backseat. Classroom organization must emphasize creating contexts for student expression and authentic interaction, tricky to do in the regimented setting of schools in which students' roles as passive learners are deeply engrained. Consciously planning for discussion can help ameliorate these difficulties; this chapter has presented several ways to do so.

4

CIVIC COMMUNICATIONS

Writing and Expression for
Civic Learning

We're talking about murders and stuff because we're writing a book . . .
We're writing a book about the murders in the city of Surrey and we had
then after we write about different murders, we had to write a short
biography on our self and had to get pictures and different stuff like that.

(Tanisha, Surrey High School)

I actually did the acceptance and lack of acceptance in the Jewish community
of homosexuals . . . I mean I am Jewish, but I haven't studied all the different
sects of Judaism. And they, their opinion is like really varied, vary widely,
just on all ends of the spectrum . . . It was really eye opening to learn that
just because it's one religion doesn't mean it's one opinion.

(Leah, Allwood High School)

When it's bad [a debate] people don't explain stuff well, or they don't give
certain information that helps it out. But if it's good, that means you did
your research, you know, you understand it and you know how to explain
it good.

(Marquan, Oak Knoll High School)

Writing and other forms of communication are civic skills that must be built
throughout a student's time in school. Social studies is a natural and vital site for
the development of these skills. Moreover, activities that center on writing and
expression provide perfect conduits for involving students actively in civic learning.
Creating and presenting a mock news conference on the civil rights movement,
writing entries for scrapbook on community problems, writing and delivering a
speech on genocide, all call for the active engagement of students with key civic

dilemmas that is at the heart of a sociocultural approach to civic learning. Such practices can effectively work the connections between students' lives, current issues, and larger civic themes.

For Tanisha, quoted above, research and writing were a holistic part of her class's investigation of community problems. Leah's description of her "social protest movement" project is an example of how students can develop research, analytical and presentation skills through investigating topics of direct personal relevance. Marquan's analysis demonstrates how students can learn what makes for an effective argument through the expressive practice of debate. For all of these students, writing and other expressive activities both developed important civic skills and brought them more actively into engagement with the large civic themes and questions that undergirded the curricular redesign effort described in this book.

This chapter considers the why and how of writing and expression for civic learning. Beginning with an exploration of what writing and other forms of expression might have to do with civic learning, the chapter examines the links between these crucial skills and civic competence and engagement. Drawing upon student writing and expressive activities in the study classrooms, this chapter illustrates how valuable civic skills can be cultivated alongside and through activities that draw students into deeper consideration of enduring civic questions.

Why Writing and Expression for Civic Learning in Social Studies?

> Democratic leadership certainly requires clear thinking about public matters, but it also involves the communication of our thoughts and actions, both vertically, to our leaders and representatives, and horizontally, with our fellow citizens.
>
> *(Battisoni, 1997, pp. 152–3)*

Writing and other forms of expression are both communicative and analytical tools, building citizens' capacities to think through and express themselves on public issues. This section describes how writing and expressive activities can be a key aspect of building students' civic communication skills, increasing analytical capacities important to engaged citizenship, and preparing citizens who are ready for college and career.

Communication as an essential civic skill. Communication is essential for meaningful civic participation. Active citizenship involves communication, both with those working directly in government and with fellow citizens. Civic participation involves a variety of skills: writing, critical thinking, and expressive forms of communication.

Writing can be a critical aspect of civic participation. Writing letters, keeping meeting minutes, taking notes, all come into play when people take an active part in civic life. Stotsky writes, writing has been as much a part of the history of democratic self-government as reading, and is as essential as public speaking . . . as local self-government developed, so too did the kind and amount of writing that people needed to do as citizens. Today this writing ranges from letters to editors and letters of inquiry or opinion to legislators to the many kinds of writing, such as agendas and minutes of meetings, needed for organizing and maintaining democratically run citizen boards and other voluntary civic or political organization.

(Stotsky, 1990, p. 72)

Indeed, Thomas Jefferson listed writing as one of his primary objectives for public education, noting that the citizen needed to be able to "calculate for himself, and to express and preserve his ideas, his contracts, and accounts, in writing" (Jefferson, in Peterson, 1960, p. 239). Communication, the ability to express one's ideas to others, is also vital for a vibrant participatory democracy. Giving a public speech, exchanging ideas in a meeting, talking with representatives, are all aspects of empowered civic participation.

Communication for expanding thinking, critical analysis, and persuasive ability. The development of these capacities goes hand in hand with the development of critical thinking skills and the cultivation of deeper understandings of complex issues. As Peter Elbow wrote, "Writing is a way to end up thinking something you couldn't have started out thinking" (1973, p. 15). Writing promotes understanding of complex topics. Goggin notes,

It is well known that writing is thinking. Writing and content, furthermore, are inseparable. After all, writers must write about something. Thus it seems reasonable to conclude that writing in any content area will provide, above all, opportunities for students to clarify their thinking about a subject. In short, students who write about topics of whatever kind usually understand them better.

(Goggin, 1985, p. 170)

Or, as teacher Jill Tenney described her use of writing as a means of engaging students with the essential questions [EQs] of the course, "hopefully by the end of that theme they would come out with a clear understanding of those EQs."

Writing, and the research that often goes along with it, is essential for the development of students' critical capacities. Wolk states,

The purpose of social studies is to help children participate in civic life. Those issues cannot be understood by merely memorizing names, dates, and places, and our civic responsibility does not begin and end at the ballot box every four years. Rather, it requires an active, deliberative, and critical mind to inform out voting and decision making.

(Wolk, 2003, p. 102)

Students develop these critical capacities through the wrestling with evidence and argument and the struggle to express oneself clearly that are part of written and expressive activities.

Writing as an essential part of college and career readiness. Citizenship preparation has long been associated with the preparation of young people to become contributing members of society as adults. The newly developed Common Core State Standards for English Language Arts & Literacy in History/Social Studies, adopted in 2010 by 47 states, the District of Colombia, and Guam (http://nasbe.org/index.php/downloads/common-core/441-adoptiontimelinescommon core) emphasize writing, research, and analysis. The new standards connect college and career readiness to citizenship skills, stating,

> the skills and understandings students are expected to demonstrate have wide applicability outside the classroom or workplace. Students who meet the Standards . . . reflexively demonstrate the cogent reasoning and use of evidence that is essential to both private deliberation and responsible citizenship in a democratic republic.
>
> *(Common Core State Standards Initiative, n.d.)*

The Common Standards assert that students should develop literacy skills in their history/social studies courses, competencies essential to "responsible citizenship" in a participatory democracy. The 10 College and Career Readiness Standards for Literacy in History/Social Studies 6–12, shown in Box 4.1, describe benchmarks that are in alignment with the goals of this project.

BOX 4.1 COLLEGE AND CAREER READINESS STANDARDS FOR WRITING IN HISTORY/SOCIAL STUDIES, GRADES 6–12

Text Types and Purposes

1. Write arguments to support a substantive claim with clear reasons and relevant and sufficient evidence.
2. Write informative/explanatory texts to convey complex information clearly and accurately through purposeful selection and organization of content.
3. Write narratives to convey real or imagined experiences, individuals, or events and how they develop over time.

Production and Distribution of Writing

4. Produce writing in which the organization, development, substance, and style are appropriate to task, purpose, and audience.
5. Strengthen writing as needed by planning, revising, editing, rewriting, or trying a new approach.
6. Use technology, including the Internet, to produce, publish, and interact with others about writing.

Research to Build Knowledge

7. Perform short, focused research projects as well as more sustained research in response to a focused research question, demonstrating understanding of the material under investigation.
8. Gather relevant information from multiple print and digital sources, assess the credibility and accuracy of each source, and integrate and cite the information while avoiding plagiarism.
9. Write in response to literary or informational sources, drawing evidence from the text to support analysis and reflection as well as to describe what they have learned.

Range of Writing

10. Write routinely over extended time frames (time for research, reflection, and revision) and shorter time frames (a single sitting or a day or two) for a range of tasks, purposes, and audiences.

These new standards set high goals for students' literacy achievement in social studies/history. They focus on constructing and supporting an argument, conducting research projects, and familiarity with a range of writing tasks. The social studies, as Beyer points out, "provides natural opportunities to teach writing. Whenever we ask students to write we have the opportunity to show them how to engage in the various skills that constitute this complicated process" (1982, p. 104).

Writing and expression to develop historical empathy. In addition, writing and expressive activities provide a way for students to develop empathy "for a condition, group of people or period of time" (Beyer, 1982, p. 103). Later in this chapter I will describe an expressive project, the Civil Rights Broadcast, in which students took on the roles of historical figures. Such expressive activities connect students to historical events, cultivating their "ability to see and judge the past in its own terms by trying to understand the mentality, frames of reference, beliefs, values, intentions, and actions of historical agents," to "view the world as it was seen by the people in the past without imposing today's values" (Yilmaz, 2007, p. 331).

Developing a Civic Writing and Expression Strand for the New Curriculum

The study team agreed that writing and expression should be a key part of the new curriculum, both to hone these essential skills, and as a way to facilitate student connection of themes to history. In consultation with a trained writing coach, the team collaboratively developed a focus on writing fluency and argumentation to be threaded throughout the year. Box 4.2 shows the results of this process.

BOX 4.2 WRITING AND EXPRESSING CIVICS IN THE NEW CURRICULUM

Strand 2:

Writing and Expressing Civics—Using Writing and Expression in a the Problem-Posing Civics Approach

Goals for Students:
- To use writing to connect the curriculum to students' lives and civic experiences, to build upon students' own experiences with civic life, including daily experiences with civic institutions and their agents
- To consider key issues and controversies in civic life through writing
- To write more and be able to use writing creatively
- To use writing to express opinions and persuade
- To learn to use evidence in writing
- To build skills of analysis and critique.

OVERVIEW: After reviewing the many different genres of writing and expression, our research team concluded that development of persuasive writing skills be the concentrated area of focus throughout the school year. As Jill stated, "persuasion is the ultimate form of civic expression."

In addition to focusing on persuasive writing throughout the year, teachers agreed that the use of a social studies journal will be an additional form of writing/expression implemented in the classroom throughout the year. The

---

journal will attempt to link students' personal experiences to the concepts in the course.

FREQUENCY AND METHOD: Persuasive piece—There will be one major persuasive piece per marking period. Each persuasive piece should somehow revisit the big questions underlying the focus of each thematic marking period. Social studies journal—Students will write in their social studies journals 2–5 times/week in response to teacher-initiated prompts. These journal prompts will be recorded and will draw upon students' civic experiences. Each marking period, teacher will choose two topics that will require more formal paragraph response from students, to which teachers will respond with appropriate feedback.

The remainder of this chapter will focus on the written and expressive activities used in the study classrooms, exploring both why such activities are civically beneficial and how they can be effectively incorporated into the social studies curriculum. First, we will consider how writing was used in the focal classrooms to get class sessions started, providing ready tie-in between larger themes and questions and the day's activities. We will then take a look at expressive activities in which students plan and participate in practices, such as skits and simulations, that draw upon their creative and dramatic capacities. Then, we turn to an examination of written and oral activities, such as persuasive essays and debates, designed to hone students' skills of persuasion and argumentation. The next section examines the use of essays to hone the critical literacy skills of writing and thinking about essential questions. Finally, we will consider the writing and expression that take place as students investigate a social movement of their choosing.

Writing and Expression in the Study Classrooms

Getting Started: Do-Nows and Social Studies Journals

> "So far this year we studied electoral politics/civics, economics, conflict/ resolution. Each relates to the lives *you* live. How?"
> *(On the board in Mr. Brooks' classroom when students enter the room)*

Writing was an essential part of the focal classrooms from the beginning of each class session. Opening classes with a written response to a key question, sometimes called a "do-now," allowed teachers to get the class started on a focused note. The writing could then lead into a discussion or other activity, preparing students for the activity to come. Social studies journals were also used as a way to connect students' lives and experiences to the curriculum. They were used to bracket a complex idea, particularly in relation to essential questions. They were employed to prepare students for an upcoming discussion or other activity. Ms. Tenney's list of do-now questions in Box 4.3 shows the trajectory of the year.

BOX 4.3 MS. TENNEY'S DO-NOW QUESTIONS FOR THE YEAR

1. What does our government do for us?
2. Define government.
3. Lunches or backpacks? Which one should we investigate further?
4. If you could speak to the president for five minutes, what issues would you want to discuss and what advice would you give on those issues?
5. Did the political quiz results surprise you? Why/why not?
6. Which of the Constitution principles do you believe is the most important for our government to protect in today's society?
7. Should the electoral college be stopped?
8. What are the duties and responsibilities of a good American citizen?
9. What can the three little pigs teach us about decision making?
10. How can athletes' salaries be so high when salaries for other occupations that are clearly more important are so much lower?
11. Who controls gas prices in the U.S.?
12. 1—Define problem, 2—Is it realistic?, 3—Three plans.
13. Which of the three types of business organizations is most beneficial to society? Why?
14. Child labor exists today. How should we as American citizens respond to these unfair practices?
15. How much control should the government have over the economy?
16. How much control should the government have over the economy? (Relation to New Deal.)
17. If you lived in the 1930s would you support or be a critic of the New Deal? Why?
18. What connections do you see between FDR's New Deal and Johnson's Great Society?
19. What is America's role in world conflicts? Should it be action or inaction? Why/why not?
20. Should the U.S. have alliances? Why? If so, who?
21. Have you ever experienced or seen bullying? How would you react?
22. Are the Four Freedoms relevant in today's society? In what context?
23. What is the purpose of 9/20 speech? How would you feel as a U.S. citizen on 9/20?

24. Which battle in the Pacific Theater do you feel is the most important? Why?
25. Voices of Atomic Bomb survivors—Give three arguments from the perspective of the person in your article.
26. Explain the international consequences of WWII for allied and axis powers? Was the war worth it?
27. What caused the Cold War and what policy did the U.S. maintain?
28. How did the Chinese Communists gain control of China? How did the U.S. respond?
29. How did McCarthy play on American fears of Communism?
30. Should Kennedy have gone through with the CIA's plan to invade Cuba? Could or should he have done things differently?
31. Make a KWL chart. What do you know about JFK's assassination? What do you want to know?
32. What characteristics define a good president? Are some more important than others? Why?
33. Have you ever argued with someone over possession of an object that was important to you? What prolonged the conflict? How was it or how could it have been resolved?
34. If Christianity, Judaism, and Islam are so similar, why is there so much fighting in the Middle East?
35. Why were the Camp David accords an important step toward peace in the Middle East?
36. It's September 12, 2001. You are president of the U.S. What do you do? What do you say to the American people? What is your plan of action?
37. After a war, should the U.S. leave the country they were fighting in, and not occupy it anymore?
38. What/who is an American?
39. If you were a native born American in the 1800s, how would you have reacted to the influx of immigrants?
40. Should the U.S. have a closed or open door policy towards immigration? Why/why not?
41. "The New Colossus"—What is the poem about? What are some words or phrases that make you think this?
42. p. 197—Critical Thinking vs. Nativists.
43. How did the 1965 Act change immigration to the U.S.?
44. What legislation was passed in the 1990s? How was legal and illegal immigration affected?
45. Read the "Virtual Fence" article. Can this solve the illegal immigration problem? Why? If not, what do you think should be done to secure our borders?

46. If you were the next president, how would you handle immigration issues?
47. Define migration. How is it different from immigration?
48. Why are people forced to leave their homelands? How?
49. "Nor shall private property be taken for public use, without just compensation." 1—What amendment in the Bill of Rights contains this phrase? 2—What power does this give government? (What is it called?)
50. Describe the picture.
51. Activities in the past 24 hours. Evidence.
52. Are you treated in a certain way because of your gender? Explain.
53. What message is Sojourner trying to promote?
54. What do you know about current laws regarding abortion in the U.S.? Write a list of terms, ideas, concepts you associate with the legislation and public debate around the issue of abortion.
55. What difference do you note in girls' and boys' sports? What is Title IX? Why did it originate? Do you think it is fair? Explain.
56. What issues motivated Mexican American activists to protest? Why did the various groups use different approaches?

As noted earlier, the team developed a plan for journal writing designed to help students both develop writing fluency and to connect their own experiences and the essential questions to the content of the course. Box 4.4 shows how the team described the approach to journal writing during the summer workshop before implementation.

BOX 4.4 THE SOCIAL STUDIES JOURNAL

During the school year, students will be asked to write informally 2–5 times weekly on topics related to the essential questions of the course. The social studies journal will be a place where students can connect their own experiences and opinions to the course themes and content. Teachers can assign students quick writing topics at the beginning or end of class, for homework, or at any other point in the day where it makes sense to do so. At the end of each marking period, students will choose two selections from the journal to write up in a more formal format. The journal will be collected 1–2 times per marking period and assessed for completion using a nonletter grade. Teachers will respond to the ideas expressed in the journal, rather than correcting errors.

While the teachers varied in their strict adherence to these goals, all used writing prompts at the beginning of class in this way.

Jessica, in Allwood, described the beginning of a typical class session:

Jessica: Well, we start with a do-now.
Interviewer: What's a do-now?
Jessica: A do-now? It'd be a question on the board. We had a journal actually that we'd keep in the class. Every day we'd write down the questions and we'd do an answer and then we'd discuss it . . . It was always like an open discussion.

For Jessica and her classmates, the opening do-now, a writing prompt that connected the day's lesson to larger themes and issues, was part of the daily routine and ensured that each class session would begin with students thinking hard about a course-related issue.

To get class started. Journals were a fluid, responsive tool. They could be used as opener, closer, to evaluate an argument, to connect a topic to current events. In the example below, Mr. Banks at Oak Knoll High School used a writing prompt to segue into discussion of a key civic issue.

On the board: "USII Do Now: 3/10/08—Take out "Century: Civilians at War." —Respond in notes: "Do you think the targeting of civilians can be justified during WWII?"

Mr. Banks used this writing prompt to engage students in the dilemma of morality during war as an entry point for a lesson on the dropping of the atomic bomb on Hiroshima. In this way, students have a stake in the information, a personal interest in the topic before moving into a traditional lecture. It also gave them a chance to practice reflective writing, even in a lesson largely dedicated to listening.

For students to connect the topic to their own lives. Journal prompts were used to connect students own lives to the topic of the day. Samantha in Surrey went through her social studies journal with the interviewer, describing the do-nows Mr. Brooks assigned:

Um, I think I have some here that he made us do. Like this is a do-now. Like we had to take ten minutes, like "How do you deal with threats?" And things like that. It could be like possible conflicts, court cases, parenthood, graduation, grades, etcetera.

Journals provide a place for students to make a quick connection between their own lives and the topic at hand. Mr. Brooks describes,

I try to have them writing every day. We ask them a question about themselves about their lives, that sort of thing. What would you do and how do you feel about this. And then we're actually voicing them from very early on, they're getting used to voicing their opinions . . . Writing civics, they did that more or less early in the year with actually writing about politics and issues and what they see or how they fit in.

Ms. Tenney agreed:

Most of the civic- social studies journal entries have to do with their opinion, their own experiences. Asking them to define them, but also when we talk about community problems, that they're bringing their own experiences in
. . .
Because really, through the general questions you can ask a question directly related to themselves on whatever topic that you're talking about.

Journals effectively bridged the gap between students' experiences and larger civic issues.

To scaffold and deepen students' consideration of complex ideas. Social studies journals were a useful way to guide students' pre- and post-lesson consideration of a complex topic. Brief reflective writing, both at the beginning and end of a class session, provided students with time and space to grapple with issues that required thought, and connect historical events to essential questions. Ms. Tenney described this process:

I'll ask them a question, and you know usually it will be before we teach the content, just to get their opinion. And then I'll ask them to look back at their answer, or if we go over the answer at the end of class sometimes they amend what they wrote, and write like a second paragraph to the question.

For example, in Allwood, during the Conflict and Resolution unit, Ms. Tenney's student teacher used her do-now as a warm up for the structured conversation. The classroom scene below depicts this practice.

The students quietly complete their journal for the day: "Should Kennedy have gone through with the CIA's plan to invade Cuba? Could or should he have done things differently?"
Ms. Tenney's student teacher, Ms. Monroe, is running the class today. She quietly assigns numbers to split the class into groups for a structured conversation as the students write in their social studies journal for about 10 minutes. The writing draws to a close, and Ms. Monroe calls for the class's attention. They discuss the prompt briefly, before she splits the class into groups for the structured conversation.
After the discussion activity, Ms. Monroe then addressed the class, saying "Okay, good job guys. Go back to your seats and take out your journals.

(Students set the desks back the original way.) These are the statements (she passes out a handout). Some we went over today, others we didn't. In your journals, react to one of them about the U.S. role in conflict and resolution.

In this example, individual written reflection was used to bolster students' consideration of a complex key question, when should the United States go to war, in relation to a particular event, the Bay of Pigs.

This use of journal writing was particularly effective for helping students to grapple with a unit's essential questions. Ms. Tenney described,

> One of the things that I liked to do and I kind of did it with economics, and I'm kind of doing it with conflict/resolution, is ask the same journal questions throughout the marking period, or throughout the whole big unit. So, you know, "Is war just?" At first they're all going to say no, or you know, yes, or whatever they're going to say. And then after World War I ask the same question, and after World War II ask the same question, and see how over time that changes based on the knowledge that they now have. And I did the same thing with economics, I asked the same question a few different times, you know, after we learned something . . . Well one of the things was "What is the role of government in the economy?" We asked that over and over again, because we went from you know, Hoover, which was you know, and the 20s' presidents' laissez-faire, to FDR, to Great Society, to Reagan, so that question was asked like four times. And then "How does the economy affect me, and how do I affect the economy?" And kind of seeing like, over time, like, you know, if the government spends all of this money on, let's say guns, then how does butter get affected, and how do I get affected, and you know, kind of seeing that perspective over time, too. So, I mean, you know, with those questions asked several times, I think they could really go back and have strong opinions, once you get to that final, you know, assignment, or essay, or Take-a-Stand, or whatever it is, and I'm kind of doing the same thing with conflict/resolution. And one of the questions is "What is the role of America in the world, action vs. inaction," so I'm going to ask that question several times, and then "is war just?" is probably the other question that I'll ask a few times, you know, just so that they get some perspective over time.

This use of writing, as Ms. Tenney explained, helped to anchor the curriculum in the essential question under study, maintaining connection to the key civic issues underlying the historical study. As she described, students will have grappled in writing with the question "Is war ever just?" several times and in relation to several different time periods, tackling the question in an essay.

As preparation for another activity. Teachers found the journals to be useful to prepare students for another activity. Ms. Tenney described,

And then with the journals, sometimes we'll talk about it as a group, sometimes we'll pair-share, sometimes we'll turn that into later on some kind of Take-a-Stand or Socratic seminar, so now they're able to provide opportunities for students to you know, discuss and consider those key issues, and realize that you know, people disagree with you. And some people agree with you.

At Allwood, Ms. Tenney used the journals as a way to have students think about the various civic problems the class was considering for selection, prior to a full class debate on the issue. Describing how she anticipated making the final problem selection, she reflected,

What I figure we'd do is have a class debate. I have them, in their social studies journal, write which one, out of the two that the class voted for, did they feel was . . . you know . . . a valid argument and had a lot of support and they could accomplish or solve. I figured what we were going to is debate, so we have two sides and from there, choose one. So, hopefully, through a debate, they can define their issue a little more. And, if there are any holes in it, be able to identify them.

She also used the journals as an introduction to the "Meet the Candidates" activity described later in this chapter. She noted,

I had them write first in their journals. Like, what you think you are and why. And then, we did like a little quiz to give us an idea, kind of, about some issues. Then, we talked about some broader issues, and what they would feel. Then, we identified it as "is it conservative or is it liberal?" Some of them got it, and then, some of them were like "what?"

Mr. Brooks and Mr. Banks used journal prompts in this way as well, using them for student brainstorming on problems they could take on for the action research project that I will describe in the next chapter.

Creative Expressions: Taking a Role, Playing a Part

Some of the most effective expressive activities were those that required students to take a role or play a part. These activities involved students in research, writing, and expression in ways that were engaging, fun, and memorable. Two examples of such activities were a candidates' forum and a civil rights era newscast, both conducted at Allwood High School.

Candidates' forum. It was October, a time when most U.S. II classes might be in the midst of reading about the Progressive Era. Ms. Tenney's students, in the middle of their Government theme, were researching positions on healthcare, war, and education of the numerous candidates participating in the primaries leading up to the 2008 election.

It was early in the 2008 election cycle and many candidates filled the airwaves with their positions on civic issues, providing Ms. Tenney with a perfect opportunity to have her students participate in a candidate roundtable. With their talking points in front of them, students expressed their positions on these key civic issues, questioned each other, and responded in character.

> The students enter the room, excited and chattering. As they sat down in a circle they took out folded over sheets of paper with their "names": Barack Obama, Chris Dodd, Mike Huckabee, John McCain, Fred Thompson, Alan Keyes, Tom Tancredo, John Edwards, Dennis Kucinich, Bill Richardson, Mike Gravel, Duncan Hunter, Mitt Romney, Sam Brownback, Hillary Clinton (played by two students), Joe Biden (another two), and Ron Paul. The student playing Rudy Giuliani was absent.

As Zahir, who played Hillary Clinton, recalled,

> we would start off like Miss Tenney, she'd bring up one topic like she would say "the war in Iraq" and then people would just go around saying, "Hi. I'm Barack Obama and I believe that blah-blah-blah." And "I'm Hillary Clinton blah-blah-blah." After we all introduced each other, people like said their candidate's opinions about it and someone opposing that would be like "Well, I don't believe that. I believe that." It was really fun. We got to see how people argue from their candidates' point of view.

At the end of the school year, Ryan recalled this activity from the Fall,

> we each had to research and pick our presidential candidate before nobody was out of the race or anything. And we researched their key points, their arguments. And then we had to present two minutes, deliver your key points, to people in the audience so they knew, and then the second part was, we threw out an issue, and we'd debate it as we were the candidates. Which I thought was really cool, even though you didn't agree with the candidate, still like, you had a presidential debate. Which I thought was cool. Because you got to see like, even as a teenager, what these people were thinking, what direction our country could go . . . it was really, really cool because it was very involved. And it really informed people I think, in our class, about the election. Because after that, when somebody would drop out, everyone would know who, because you got people interested in it. Which I thought was really cool, because usually before that they probably didn't even know there was an election.

Raj also remembered the activity eight months after the event. At the time of the interview he was still following the election, reflecting that,

> even though I won't get to vote in this year's, like I still want to find out like what like the candidate thinks about on certain issues and how they're different or similar with mine. And just to see like how the whole process works out.

Taking part in an expressive activity in which they researched and took on the role of a candidate involved students directly in current civic issues in a memorable way while building their expressive capacities.

Civil Rights Broadcast. One expressive activity in which writing was an "integral part of the learning part of the teaching learning process rather than just an interruption" (Beyer, 1982, p. 104) was the Civil Rights News Broadcast created by students in the fourth semester. Part of the Social Change theme described in Chapter 2, Table 2.2, the Civil Rights News Broadcast was partially developed during the summer workshop. The team designed the activity, described in Box 4.5, for the third marking period.

BOX 4.5 THE NEWSCAST/ROUNDTABLE/TALKSHOW FORMAT

Marking Period #3 —The Newscast/Roundtable/Talkshow/Panel Format

Students will take on a particular perspective/character and write an opening statement presenting their character's perspective on the marking period's underlying questions. The ensuing "conversation" will take place in a roundtable/talkshow format similar to the Sunday morning news shows with opposing viewpoints. Students should familiarize themselves with effective speech techniques used by people when responding to pressing questions. Members of the research team will be on hand for the roundtable event to pose questions to the students.

In this assignment, then, students wrote and presented a "news broadcast" of a civil rights related topic as a contemporary, "news-of-the-day" broadcast, bringing research, writing, and oral communication to bear on a pivotal historical topic linked to essential questions. Box 4.6 shows the assignment, further developed by Ms. Tenney and her student teacher for use in the classroom. It calls for students to grapple with a topic and transform it into a news broadcast, turning their historical research into an interactive enactment in which students took on a historical character and responded to questions from his or her perspective.

BOX 4.6 THE NEWSCAST ASSIGNMENT

Civil Rights News Broadcast

You are part of a news team at a national broadcast station. Your job is to give a news broadcast about events and issues occurring across the nation. Each group will be responsible for one area below. Broadcast should last 4–5 minutes.

In your groups, each member will be responsible for a different role. If you have a group of three, you may pick any three as long as at least one role is a news anchor or reporter.

A. News Anchor: To give lead-up or background into an event.
B. Reporter: Person in the field, at the scene, seeing the action.
C. Bystander or informed citizen: To comment on what is happening.
D. Civil Rights Leader: To express views of an organization or movement.

Topics:

1. Registering voters
2. Black Muslims and Malcolm X
3. Black Power and the Black Panther Party
4. Urban violence and the SCLC
5. Busing and affirmative action
6. Race and the election of 2008
7. New Orleans

Students will take on a particular perspective/character and write an opening statement presenting their character's perspective on the marking period's underlying questions. The ensuing "conversation" will take place in a roundtable/talkshow format similar to the Sunday morning news shows with opposing viewpoints. Students should familiarize themselves with effective speech techniques used by people when responding to pressing questions. Members of the research team will be on hand for the roundtable event to pose questions to the students.

In a newscast on Black Muslims and Malcolm X, three students researched, wrote, and enacted the perspective of Malcolm X and other Black Muslim citizens in the 1960s. Reem took on the role of a member of the Black Muslims and Erica was the reporter in this excerpt:

Erica: Good morning. Would you do so kindly as to introduce yourself?

Reem: I am a follower of the Honorable Elijah Mohammad and that is all I need to say.

Erica: Alright then. When did you join the association?

Reem: I joined 20 years ago, March of 1943 to be exact.

Erica: And what prompted your allegiance to Elijah Mohammad?

Reem: My parents were killed by the members of the Klu Klux Klan. I handled this well and still looked to Mr. Kind and nonviolent protest, but when my sister was shot down by a fire hose, right next to me, I was convinced to change my ways. Her mangled body, bones broken by the impact of the hose, told me that nonviolence would not solve anything.

Erica: I am sorry about your sister, sir, but do you believe that violence is the only way to convince the society of your equal rights?

Reem: No, I do not believe that.

Erica: Then what do you believe?

Reem: I believed that when we are violently attached by mobs or armed gunmen it is quite all right to use violence to defend ourselves. This is what we have been taught by the great messenger Elijah.

. . . *Later in the same newscast* . . .

Erica: Alright then. Our next guest is a well known person by the name of Malcolm X. Malcolm X was born on May 19, 1925. Also known as El-Hajj Malik, he was an American Black Muslim minister and a spokesman for the Nation of Islam. After leaving the Nation of Islam in 1964 he made the pilgrimage, the Hajj, to Mecca and became a Sunni Muslim. He also founded the Muslim Mosque, Inc. and the Organization of Afro-American Unity. Although most of his life was dedicated to the Nation of Islam, he recently broke away from it. Please welcome Malcolm X.

Rupal: Good morning.

Erica: Before you get started, would you mind giving a short biography for the people who do not know you?

Rupal: I'd be delighted to. I was born on May 19, 1925 in Omaha, Nebraska. My mother's name is Louise Norton and my father is Earl. I used to be an avid supporter of Marcus Garvey, a Black Nationalist leader. My father's civil rights activism prompted death threats from a white supremacist organization, and two years later his mutilated body was found lying across the town's trolley tracks. Although this incident sent my mother into depression, I remained assimilated with the whites. When I expressed my interest in becoming an attorney my professor, a white man, denounced my dreams, saying that a Black man cannot possibly get such a position.

Erica: Did you join the Black Nationalists after that?

Rupal: No. I dropped out of school, spent some time in Boston, Massachusetts working various odd jobs, and then traveled to Harlem, New York where I committed petty crimes. By 1942 I was coordinating various narcotics and gambling rings. I was arrested and convicted on burglary charges in 1946. It was during the period of self-enlightenment that my brother Reginald visited and discussed his recent conversion to the Muslim religious organization the Nation of Islam. Intrigued, I studied the teachings of the Nation of Islam leader Elijah Muhammad. Muhammad taught that white society actively worked to keep African Americans from empowering themselves and achieving political, economic and social success. Among other goals, the Nation of Islam fought for a state of their own, separate from one inhabited by white people. By the time I was paroled in 1953 I was a devoted follower, with the new surname "X."

This excerpt demonstrates students' understanding of a different time period, various viewpoints from that time period, and the complex issue of racism and the struggle for racial equality. It also shows students' abilities to communicate these ideas with a good degree of precision and descriptiveness, and to turn historical research into understandable text and portrayal. Creating characters and dialogue forced the students to be precise about the historical content while considering the essential question of how social change occurs. Writing and presenting the newscast built students' creative, descriptive, narrative, expressive, and persuasive skills, and fostered a classroom setting in which students shared different perspectives on key civic questions, such as the questions about how far one should go to fight injustice underlying this unit on social change.

Arguing a Point: Debates and Persuasive Essays

The team decided that persuasive writing was central to civic writing and the expressive skills we wanted students to develop. Debates, essays, and letters all build students' persuasive writing and expressive skills. In this project, such activities developed students' capacities to express and defend an opinion, use evidence, and analyze the arguments offered by others, all skills promoted by the new Common Standards for Literacy in History/Social Studies, as noted earlier.

Debates. Debates were public displays of persuasive skill that both demonstrated and honed students' understandings of what made for a compelling argument. Mr. Banks used debates regularly in his classroom, giving students time to research and prepare, come in with prepared statements in which they cited evidence, and then following up the debate with a writing assignment. In December, while his classes were studying prohibition, Mr. Banks assigned his students the debate topic of whether illegal substances should be regulated, outlawed or made legal, a question that bridged historic and current civic issues.

On the day we observed, six students were participating in the debate. They came prepared with opening and closing statements and facts to support their opinions. The rest of the class was ready to observe the debate while filling out their "debate critique sheets," so they had the material they needed to write an editorial on the debate topic. Mr. Banks' students entered the room and took their seats. Six students sat down in the middle of the room in two rows of desks, three desks per room, facing each other, ready to begin their debate on government regulation of drugs and alcohol. Eduardo began to read from a typed sheet he had placed on his desk.

> Eduardo: I believe the U.S. government has the right to regulate drugs. Any drug that is harmful to one's health should be prohibited. Some that have medical uses, such as marijuana, should be regulated. I have found in my research that it has medical uses.

Eduardo continued to read his carefully prepared statement, taking over a minute to open the debate. He had evidence to support his points and his argument was coherent. His classmates seemed to notice this immediately. "That was good as hell!" exclaimed a student sitting next to me.

Debates showcased the quality of students' research and written preparation and their persuasive powers, and, as Eduardo's classmates registered, provided peers with a graphic illustration of the effectiveness of evidence and coherent argumentation. Percy, a student who transferred to Oak Knoll from a school in a nearby low-income urban center, described a good debater,

> When you know what you're talking about. Like there are people they'll just write and they won't really give any examples or be able to back up what they said. And that just kind of when you read it it's like wow. It's stupid kind of. When you could actually back it up with examples and stuff like that? It's good. I think that makes a really strong argument.

Malcolm, reflecting on his own lackluster debate performance, made the connection between evidence and preparation and performing well in the debate.

> I definitely could have prepared better. But it was an interesting topic to do. I could a got more points, more information. If I would have gotten more information on it, it would have been better . . . I mean, half, half of my little debate team was a kind of a little rocky, like off, because of me, but they brought themselves back, they kind of cleaned up the whole, the whole thing . . . when it's bad, it's as if people don't, like, they don't explain stuff well, or they don't give certain information that helps it out. But if it's good, that means you did your research, you know, you understand it, and you know how to explain it good.

A good debater, according to Malcolm, was well informed, had evidence, and was able to explain things well. Research was part of this. As he recounted, describing the successful debaters, "They did a lot of research. I know about a couple people they did a lot of research, they were debating back and forth. They was doing real good, they knew what they was talking about."

When a student was not well prepared, it was both bothersome and noticeable to peers. Eric reflected,

> other people on the other side just get me mad, because they was saying dumb, dumb. I mean, like it's your opinion, but come on. It was stupid! . . . I think, it wasn't that it was mean, or ignorant, I mean it was their opinion, but I thought that they didn't know what they was talking about. They didn't know what it was about. It was like, you judging somebody but you don't know about them. They didn't know about the subject but they was saying stuff.

The public practice of debate helped students to develop research and expressive skills, as well as honing their abilities to judge the arguments, evidence and persuasiveness of their classmates.

Persuasive letters, speeches, and essays. The team focused on students' persuasive writing through essays, letters and speeches. During the summer workshop, the research team decided to integrate these forms of writing into the curriculum, as shown in Box 4.7.

BOX 4.7 PERSUASIVE LETTER, SPEECH, AND ESSAY DESCRIPTIONS

Marking Period #1—The Persuasive Letter

Students will work to develop the skills necessary to write a persuasive letter, which will be connected back to the big questions guiding the economics concepts.

The letter will be graded according to a rubric that will assess: format, proper greetings, paragraphs—introduces writer and problem, explains opinion in detail, and calls for action; evidence as demonstrated by at least two major points; inclusion of the opposing opinion; and calls for action/ solution to the problem. Our research team may provide written responses to your students' letters.

Marking Period #2—The Persuasive Speech

Students will study examples of persuasive speeches throughout the marking period in the context of conflicts and resolutions and discuss the merits of various examples of speech. As their final assignment, students will be asked to write/perform a speech pertaining to one of the major underlying questions of the marking period, i.e., "is war justified?"

Marking Period #4—The Five-Paragraph Essay

After the fourth marking period, students will revisit the question underlying the instruction and inquiry from the term: "Are all Americans equal?" Students will revisit the skills used in earlier forms of persuasive writing to craft an introductory paragraph consisting of a thesis statement that will foreshadow the major arguments of the essay. The essay should have three paragraphs following the introduction, each with a topic sentence, supporting evidence, and a closing sentence. These paragraphs should build to support the thesis of the essay. Essays should conclude with a conclusion paragraph that restates the thesis and summarizes the main idea in each paragraph. The essay should have a zinger of a closing statement that effectively persuades.

The new national standards place persuasive writing at the center of the objectives for students in social studies/history writing.

In the Fall, during the Economics theme, students wrote persuasive letters to President Bush about the economy and other issues. Lalit's letter in Box 4.8 shows how he has learned to use evidence to make an argument.

BOX 4.8 LALIT'S PERSUASIVE LETTER

October 2nd, 2007

Dear Mr. President,

I am writing to you because I strongly feel that the economic issues and problems in this country are becoming worse day by day. A few of the problems that I believe are quite crucial and worth thinking about are retirement savings and social security, energy, and public debt. If we do not act upon these issues soon, they can get really out of hand and we won't be able to fix them or do anything about them.

I believe that the Americans are not planning ahead and aren't saving enough money for their retirement by themselves. Since these people are relying on Social Security for their future, they are putting Social Security in financial trouble at this moment. The likely outcome of this problem will be that the political pressure from powerful entrenched interests will most likely bury any chance of reform in the future. Any real institutional reform will most probably be put off for at least about another five or ten years or may be even longer, limiting the possible outcomes to more extraordinary measures such as higher taxes or lower benefits.

In addition, the problem of retirement savings and social security, another problem that needs to be taken care of is energy. The increasing use of computers and electronic technology makes the impact of increasing prosperity, which also increases the energy use, worse. At the same time, the efficiency as not as nearly good as where it should be compared to how much energy is being used. The most likely outcome of this will be that the energy supplies won't ever run out completely, not even nonrenewable sources such as oil. However, they will increase in cost and will become more expensive over time.

Public debt is another issue to think about and solve quickly. The United States is under a huge debt at this moment because the Federal government cannot keep spending under control. Many costly governments have concentrated benefits and diffuse costs. That meaning that the people who benefit end up much better off, while the costs are spread out over a large number of taxpayers.

These problems are very serious and can cause great damage in the future if they are not fixed or acted upon soon enough. I hope you take a look at these problems very carefully and sort them out as soon as possible. Thank you for listening to my concerns.

Sincerely,
Lalit Parikh

Saria and Emily each used historical evidence to argue their own perspective on whether or not the United States was living up to promises made in the Declaration of Independence and the Bill of Rights (see Box 4.9).

BOX 4.9 SARIA AND EMILY'S PERSUASIVE LETTERS

Saria

I believe that the United States is not living up to the promises made in the Declaration of Independence or the liberties granted by the Bill of Rights because of the following reasons. When the U.S. decided to pass the Japanese

Internment, they directly went against the words of the Preamble to the Declaration of Independence. In the Preamble, the quote "We hold these truths to be self-evident, that all men are created equal, that they are endowed by their Creator with certain unalienable Rights, that among these are Life, Liberty and the pursuit of Happiness," describes how everyone is created equal and has the same exact rights as their neighbors, friends, etc.

But when the U.S. decided to put innocent Japanese Americans into unsanitary and horrible camps, they did not consider even for a second that they were depriving innocent Japanese Americans rights of Life, Liberty, and the pursuit of Happiness. When the Japanese Americans were put into camps, they were treated horribly; they were allowed to take only what they could carry to the camps, they had to line up for everything including meals, bathrooms, and laundry, and finally, they could not go back to their own homes even after the Japanese Internment was over. Thus, the United States did not live up to the promises made in the Declaration of Independence during the Japanese Internment.

Emily

The United States has made many promises that were noted in the Declaration of Independence. The country has granted liberties from the Bill of Rights. Over the past years the U.S. has grown and we have learned from our mistakes. During WWII, the second we were bombed at Pearl Harbor we assumed all Japanese living in America were also in on it. We immediately put the Japanese in internment camps. Life was hell for them and was hard to get back up. Almost 40 years later Reagan made a formal apology. I believe he looked at the situation and now saw it was wrong. Post 9/11 Bush made a statement saying he respects the Muslim people and that terrorists involved in Al Qaeda are our enemy. He didn't single out everyone in the U.S who's Muslim and put them into internment camps. As we look back on past experiences like these the U.S. has learned a lot and is giving rights and liberties to those people.

These statements show an ability to consider historical events in light of large civic questions. They also show students weighing evidence and taking positions on controversial topics. Rather than producing a memorized response to a factual question, they are drawing upon their factual knowledge to answer an open-ended question. In so doing, they are putting historical content into dynamic use, creating their own interpretations of the meaning of particular events. In doing this, they are taking part in an ongoing civic discussion of the extent to which the United

States is living up to its foundational principles and are becoming active participants in our ongoing civic discourse.

Writing and Expression to Grapple with Essential Questions.

Writing was an effective means for students to grapple deeply with the essential questions in the course and to connect historical study to the larger civic themes embedded within those questions.

Essential questions as essay prompts. One way that Ms. Tenney did this was to use essential questions as essay prompts for her unit tests.

> On the tests that they've had at the end of the unit, I've given them, one part of the test is I gave them the essential questions, which they also had as journal prompts, which we also talked about in class, and I gave them the choice to answer two of the four, or two of the five in a paragraph for their like short answer for their test. And they've all been very successful with that.

She drew a question through the discrete events and units within a theme. For example,

> Every test, we give them the same questions. But they have to answer the questions in relation to the unit they just had. So is war just? Is war just in World War I? Is war just in World War II? Is war just in Cold War? Is war just in the Middle East? Is war just with genocide where we didn't go to war necessarily in Darfur or anything like that so they had to answer the same essential question over and over again in respect to different time periods and now hopefully after the Take-a-Stand, they'll be able to kind of connect that and really weigh is war just? Should America take action or inaction knowing all the different time periods that they did or didn't.
>
> Every unit test, what I did is I gave them, every test, I gave them the same essential questions. But in order to answer the question, they had to relate it to the topic. So, if we did civil rights, they'd have the same essential question for civil rights and women's rights, but when they answered the question, they had to answer it in terms of civil rights, or they had to answer it in terms of women's rights. So they're seeing the same question now, over and over and over again, and they're writing about it in terms of different topics. So I think that also helps them formulate their own opinion on the essential questions, because even though it's the same question, depending on the topic, it may change their answer. And then throughout the theme, they may see, like, "oh wait a second, I don't really believe this." What I originally thought about the essential question, because I saw this example is one way, this example is one way. And then, hopefully by the end of that

theme, they will come out with a more clear understanding of those essential questions according to the theme topic as a whole. So that was, you know, that was my purpose in repeating and having them write on that.

The students remembered this. Janet recounted, "Essential questions come to mind first. A lot of, every test . . . every test we had to do two. They were always the same questions for every unit. But we always had to relate them back." Lalit recounted that "Every time we had tests we had to answer the open-ended questions. The . . . I forgot what they're called but there's five of them." "Essential?" "Essential questions, there we go. And they basically stayed the same."

Essential questions as part of students' social movement investigations and presentations. In Allwood, students did individual projects on a social protest movement, selecting and investigating a social protest movement of interest to them. Each student created a presentation, with an accompanying visual aide, that included a depiction of the issue, a "K–W–L" (what you *K*now, what you *W*ant to know, what you have *L*earned) chart, and answers to the theme's essential questions to the particular movement under study. Students considered the following questions as they researched a self-selected social or political movement:

- Are all Americans equal?
- How can/do Americans make social change?
- What other forces, other than individuals, shape society?
- Who has the power to make change? Do you?
- Is it ever okay to break the law? When?

Topics included the gay rights movement, the Latino rights movement, the pro-life movement, the pro-choice movement, disability rights, and many more. Janine described her project:

> I did the gay rights movement but more of gay marriage rights. So I just looked on because I'm for it of course so I just looked on like a lot of the background and what states are OK with it, which aren't . . . And then I just touched on which programs help out and then I got my friends, my friend who is gay, I got his perspective on all of it.

Students brought their own political and personal perspectives to the project, which made it memorable. Katherine described:

> Yeah honestly? I loved this project. Like I really did because the fact that we got to pick what we wanted to do like I mean like real life crises that we feel is important and I put mine on pro-life because I'm against abortion for the most part. I mean there are some situations where I feel like I guess if

you really can't afford it but going through this project I learned more than like I would have like ever thought like I would have because I thought you know, you know a lot when it comes to like I love kids and like I baby-sit for so many people. Just taking care of the kids all the time and I don't know. I never realized that when someone has an abortion, the baby's just like ripped apart in pieces, you know like. I seriously I was online, I was doing all this research and there was a thing and I thought it was like this clip of like information like to read about. And it wound up being a video. I'm telling you I sat there and I was crying watching this video. Like I couldn't it was horrible because you had people trying to stand up for pro-life that are getting beaten and like just the whole topic because people don't think, a lot of people don't think before they react and make choices until it's too late.

Kristi reflected on how choosing her own topic made the project meaningful for her, and how rare this was in school. When asked if she had ever done a similar project in school she responded:

Definitely not like this. Because a lot of ones they're just assigned and it's just like "got another project to do." So that's why I really like this because it was something we could pick that we could personally like embellish on.

Students enjoyed influencing and educating each other through their presentations and learning about a variety of topics from one another. Kate explained she "thought it was really good because it was weird to kind of influence everyone on like all the problems and not have everyone have to research everything." As with debate, the public nature of the project highlighted the importance of preparation. "I thought it was a good project," reflected Kate, "and as long as you actually prepared yourself for the presentation, you shouldn't have had a problem."

Students' social protest presentations showed the progress in thinking through historical topics in relation to the essential questions that students had made over the course of the year. As Ms. Tenney described,

I think that the last presentation that they did on social protests, we really saw some of the students who would never be comfortable standing up in front of the room in the beginning of the year, openly talk about their social protest, take questions, volunteer their own opinions, relate it to essential questions, and that was not happening, that would have never happened in September or October.

Students had developed such comfort and familiarity in working with essential questions that they were able to lead peers in consideration of them in relation to their topic. One student, Ms. Tenney related, led her peers in a consideration of the essential question for the unit in relation to her topic, Brian White and AIDS advocacy in the 1980s. Ms. Tenney described,

> she had a whole mini-lesson planned out, she wanted to ask an essential question, "Is social protest important to democracy?" She wanted to ask that question first, have everybody write, then present, then ask the question again in relation to the Brian White story, and Amy was a girl in the beginning of the year who didn't want to participate in anything that we did where she had to speak. Because she didn't like, she didn't even like to be called on in class or answer questions or do any of that . . . And to see that at the end of the year, to see her plan this lesson, with an opening and a close, it was really, it really just showed the progression of the students, with that example . . . she answered questions, the students were engaged and they were interested, and they all did the, you know, when she told them to answer the questions, they all did it, and you know, then they went back to it at the end.

As with other expressive activities described in this chapter, the social protest project allowed students to bridge their personal interests, historical study, and key civic issues while building the essential civic skills of research, analysis, writing, and expression.

Conclusion

Writing and expression, like any other skill, takes practice. As Ms. Tenney noted,

> in the beginning of the year, they were not using evidence to support their opinions in the writing, and they were also not doing it in discussion. They would say things, and I would constantly have to say, "Well, why? Why do you think that way?" And Janet even said to me at one point, "You're so mean . . . Well, I don't mean *mean*, but you don't tell us the answer. You constantly ask us 'why, why why' . . . no one does that, you constantly throw it back at us," and that's what she meant by being mean. And, you know, she was right. At the beginning of the year, I was doing that a lot more often than at the end of the year, because they weren't validating their argument, and they weren't doing it in their writing either. And I think that by practicing the writing and practicing the discussion, the two coming together and then understanding that in order for your opinion to matter, no matter if people disagree with you or if people agree with you, you need to have facts to back it up. You need to have some type of substance to base your opinion on. You can't just randomly say things. And I think that was seen in their writing throughout the year.

Students develop the skills of evidence and persuasion over time, if given the opportunity to do so in a sustained manner. Moreover, the process of doing so allows students the time and support to connect historical content to their own lives and to underlying civic issues. Both a means and a method, activities that promote written and expressive competencies are powerful tools for building engaged and capable citizens.

5

BEYOND "CURRENT EVENTS FRIDAYS"

Connecting Past to Present All Year Long

This year, from last year, focused more on like the change of America . . . focused more on like the modern problems . . . I learned a lot more . . .

(Eric, Oak Knoll High School)

It was more like the past wars, and we kind of applied it to today's war . . . that's basically what we did; we looked at Vietnam, World War II, World War I . . . applying it to today.

(Raj, Allwood High School)

In our class we are doing things that are happening or about to happen or already happened, like recently though. And in the other classes we talk about things that happened like 13,000 years ago, that don't got nothing to do with today.

(Benny, Surrey High School)

The Civic Mission of Schools 2003 report describes "classroom discussion of current events" as one of six promising approaches to civic education (Carnegie Corporation and CIRCLE, 2003). Their survey of existing research shows that such practices have direct benefits for students' civic and political knowledge and skills, civic attitudes, and political participation (Carnegie Corporation and CIRCLE, 2003, p. 22). In a context in which young people appear less interested in and aware of public affairs than ever before—in 2000 only 5% of young people ages 18–25 reported that they regularly followed public affairs (Carnegie Corporation and CIRCLE, 2003, p. 22)—such recommendations merit serious consideration.

Attention to current events may seem like a simple proposition, one that is unquestionably central to the mission of social studies. As the National Council for the Social Studies' standards state, "In essence, social studies promotes knowledge of and involvement in civic affairs" (NCSS, 2009). Yet, current events can be overlooked in social studies classrooms, or, perhaps more frequently, treated in a disconnected and superficial manner. Indeed, the very terminology of current *events* implies that what is "current" can be studied as discrete "events," occurrences that are separate and isolated from other events and from the rest of historical or social study. Indeed, some of the most common approaches to teaching current issues—students selecting a news story to summarize and report to the class on a "current events Friday" for example—reiterate the isolation of contemporary affairs from the rest of the curriculum.

In this project, the design team sought to create a more integrated approach to the study of contemporary world issues. In keeping with the design principle that "civic education should provide opportunities for students to consider and discuss key issues and controversies in civic life," our themes and questions were selected with an eye toward honing in on enduring and relevant civic themes and questions. Essential questions and a thematically organized curriculum facilitated the integration of current affairs into the U.S. History course, as will be discussed later in this chapter.

This chapter describes the importance of attention to current events both as a strategy for and an outcome of civic learning. It explores some of the reasons that social studies teachers might not use current events in their classrooms and inequalities in students' access to such instruction, considers some of the less meaningful ways that current events are commonly taught, and reviews more promising approaches. Examples from the three study schools illustrate how this project reframed traditional approaches to current events in social studies, highlighting success and challenges. No longer relegated to the sidelines, a de-contextualized curiosity, when connected to themes and essential questions current "events" can be reborn as integral to the deep consideration of ongoing civic issues, connecting history and contemporary life to make the study of both richer and more meaningful.

Why Current Events for Civic Learning?

There are a number of reasons that learning about and with current issues is important for civic learning. The Civic Mission of Schools concluded in their review of civic education practices that "When young people have opportunities to discuss current issues in a classroom setting, they tend to have greater interest in politics, improved critical thinking and communications skills, more civic knowledge, and more interest in discussing public affairs out of school" (Carnegie Corporation and CIRCLE, 2003, p. 6). Moreover, there is an equity imperative; multiple studies indicate qualitative and quantitative differences in low- and higher-income students' opportunities to experience high quality current events instruction (Kahne & Middaugh, 2008; Soule, 2006).

Fostering civic engagement. People who follow the news are more likely to be civically engaged. The Center for Information and Research on Civic Learning and Engagement's (CIRCLE) 2006 Civic and Political Health of the Nation Report describes what they call a "powerful relationship between following the news and being civically engaged," citing data showing that students who regularly use various forms of news media are more likely to take part in 19 forms of civic engagement (CIRCLE, 2006, p. 5). There also appears to be a connection between students' study of current events inside their school classrooms and their out-of-school attention to current issues (Chapman, 1997; Education World, 2010). The National Center for Education Statistics, reporting on the 1996 National Household Educational Survey of 55,838 households, explained that,

> 65 percent of students who took at least one course [incorporating national issues] during the last 2 years reported their interest in politics and national issues increased "some" or "a good deal" as a result . . . A higher percentage of students who took a course incorporating national issues in both years said their interest increased as a result. Twenty-nine percent of students took a course in both the current and previous school years and 71 percent of these students reported an increased interest in national issues as a result.
>
> *(Chapman, 1997, p. 3)*

When current events are discussed in the classroom, students appear to be more likely to follow them outside of the classroom, which, in turn, can lead to higher levels of civic engagement and awareness of current affairs.

Critical thinking and other skill building. The study of current events presents teachers with an excellent vehicle for developing students' critical thinking capacities as well as their reading, writing, listening and expressive skills. As Pescatore explains,

> Rarely, if ever, are social studies students presented with a complex issue that demands research, questioning, and an awareness of various points of view and bias . . . If the textbooks often fail to deliver, current events activities can fill the void . . .
>
> *(Pescatore, 2007, p. 336)*

Open-ended, multi-faceted and emergent by definition, current issues provide teachers with material tailor made for cultivating students' higher order thinking skills. Students "build language, vocabulary, reading comprehension, critical thinking, problem solving, oral expression, and listening skills" by engaging directly in consideration of complex issues that have no ready solution (Education World, 2010). Wrestling with current issues draws upon and develops students' reading, research, expression, and listening capacities (Pescatore, 2007, p. 336).

Preparing students for life as adult citizens. Study of current events can build the "21st century competencies" touted in national educational discourse. Torney-Purta and Wilkenfeld note that "Civic education, especially when it is interactive and involves discussion of current issues, is an important way to develop the skills that young Americans need to succeed in the 21st Century workforce" (2009, p. 7). Preparing students for adult life is the explicit aim of K-12 education, and attention to national and international current events is "one indicator of preparation for adult life" (p. 20).

Preparing students to be independently thinking citizens with the ability to investigate current issues was one of Jill Tenney's central objectives. As she shared early in the project,

> I want them to think for themselves what America should do or what they should do . . . I think that they need the background and the content but that then they should formulate how they feel themselves about the current events or the issues . . . I think that is really important. Because as adults, so many adults don't think for themselves, because they don't have the background and they don't know how to think for themselves when it comes to different issues in the country, whether it's politics or current events, and I think this is an important skill for them to understand that they can have all the content and collect all of the information, and then do something with it, and come up with their own opinion, based on some reliable sources.

Engaging with current events, Torney-Purta and Wilkenfeld assert, cultivates young people's sense of efficacy and confidence in relation to social issues which translates to "a greater sense that one is able to engage one's peers outside of class in constructive discussion" (2009, p. 23).

Raising interest, bridging gaps. Current events can be used to help answer the age-old question "why are we studying this." Sandra Feldman notes that "You can use current events to help students see the relevance and importance of their studies, that history is not a 'has-been' and, perhaps most importantly, how as productive citizens they can put their education to use in 'real life'" (2004, p. 6). As Jill Tenney put it,

> some of the goals of the project and my own personal goals is to make social studies more relevant to the students' lives, and that was always one of my main purposes prior to this curriculum. And I think that has become very apparent that you can, there are those connections and the students really enjoy understanding the world that they live in through those connections and I think that because of this they'll feel that social studies or history is much more important. Because prior to this it was always, "I don't want to learn about this, it's so boring." And now if they see the connection and

how it's relevant, I think that that will encourage them . . . to really understand what's going on in the world and be more active.

Current events are interesting to students, often holding their attention (Sumrall
& Schillinger, 2004). They also help students to understand the connections
between classroom and life.

The study of current events helps to bridge gaps, both between past and present
and between students' lives and the world outside of the classroom. Lintner notes
that,

> Social studies teachers are constantly seeking ways to connect the past with
> the present, the near with the far, the familiar with the esoteric. One of the
> most powerful ways to create such connections is through the integration
> of current events into social studies lessons . . . The immediacy and relevance
> of current events in social studies classrooms is profound because they bridge
> the gap between the classroom and the outside world and can provide
> students with information they can use in their daily lives . . .
>
> *(2006, p. 101)*

Ever-changing, complex and immediate, the study of current events has the
potential to enliven and deepen the social studies curriculum, boosting its relevance
both to students' lives and to enduring civic themes and questions.

Addressing inequalities. Recent research indicates that students from lower-
income families and noncollege-bound students are less likely to experience
discussion of current events in their social studies classrooms. In a recent study of
California high school seniors, noncollege-bound students were 30% more likely
than college-bound students "to discuss social problems or current events" (Soule,
2006). A similar study conducted in Oregon found the same results, concluding
that "disadvantaged youth are not receiving opportunities in their formal education
to acquire necessary civic knowledge or skills (Oregon Civics Survey 2006)"
(Soule, 2006).

The National Alliance for Civic Education notes that,

> civic knowledge is not evenly distributed. Those who most need the power
> that comes with political skills and information are least likely to receive an
> effective civic education. For instance, two out of three of the poorest
> Americans cannot describe the political parties' attitudes toward govern-
> ment spending, whereas most wealthy Americans know exactly how the
> Democrats differ from the Republicans. This information gap helps to
> explain the difference in voter participation between rich and poor, because
> it makes no sense to vote if you lack information about the issues.

It is crucial that all students have the opportunity to discuss contemporary issues
in their social studies classrooms. Inequities in this area compound the civic

opportunity gap that results in lower levels of civic knowledge and empowerment among low-income youth and youth of color (Kahne & Middaugh, 2008).

More Difficult to Do Well Than it Might Seem

While the utility of current events for civic education may be clear, efforts to bring the study of contemporary world events into social studies classrooms often fall short of their potential. A review of research on current events teaching reveals a scattershot approach dominated by one-time lessons that approach news as novelty, encouraging episodic treatment of contemporary events without forging connections between such events and larger civic themes with historical resonance. This section describes some of these shortcomings and outlines a few of the reasons for them.

Isolating current events from the rest of the curriculum. Current events instruction is frequently separated from the rest of the curriculum, relegated to a separate day or an occasional assignment disconnected from the course content. Turner notes that,

> What teachers have sometimes done is to separate current issues and events from the rest of the curriculum, concentrate on a limited vision of what kind of current events are acceptable for students to study and know about, reduce current events to the rigid vehicle of a single news source, and turn the whole study of news into an ordeal. In other cases, they have avoided current events altogether as unplannable, unimportant, and/or unteachable.
>
> *(Turner, 1995, p.118)*

The lesson planning literature is rife with examples of current events teaching in this vein: student reports on self-selected news articles, study of a single news source or story, summarizing or reporting events with little or no analysis or context (Hass & Laughlin, 2002; Turner, 1995). Such approaches encourage the treatment of current events as isolated, one-time occurrences rather than ongoing affairs that can be examined within the context of larger course themes.

A trivializing approach. The Internet is filled with articles describing lessons for social studies classrooms that use current events. A typical example is "Twenty-five great ideas for teaching current events" from Education World (2010). The 25 lessons include such offerings as "preserving the news" ("Dissolve a milk of magnesia tablet in a quart of water, and let it stand overnight. Pour the mixture into a flat baking pan large enough to hold the news clippings that you want to preserve. Place the clippings in the solution so they're completely covered by the liquid . . .") and "A to Z adjectives" ("Each student writes the letters from A to Z on a sheet of paper. Challenge students to search the day's front page (or the entire newspaper, if your students are older) for an adjective that begins with each letter of the alphabet. Students cut the adjectives from the newspaper and paste them on their list").

These sorts of lessons do little to advance the aims of current events instruction described in the preceding section of this chapter. Trivializing the news appears to be a persistent concern for current events instruction. Indeed, Haas and Laughlin note that in 1955, Hunt and Metcalf

> described the current events movement as having the ability to introduce fresh content into the curriculum but warned there might be a tendency to focus on the trivial or emphasize reporting of news rather than the more difficult analysis and interpretation needed to link current events to the curriculum.
>
> *(Haas & Laughlin, 2000, p. 2)*

While there are significant exceptions to these sorts of recommendations for current events teaching (see The Learning Network: Teaching and Learning with the *New York Times* [http://learning.blogs.nytimes.com/] for examples of high quality current events lessons linked to essential questions and historical themes), these are eclipsed by the preponderance of recommendations urging teachers to use news as a filler, encouraging single-use lessons that might pique student interest but are not an integral part of the social studies curriculum.

Not enough time, too controversial. Teachers may avoid sustained and critical attention to current events for various reasons beyond the lack of availability of good lesson recommendations. Recent national and state mandates leave less time overall for social studies teaching (Mitsakos & Ackerman, 2009). Current events can be controversial; their use in the classroom has been questioned and restricted at various points in recent history (Sharp, 2009). Teachers can face strong criticism for leading students into deep investigation of unresolved and contentious current issues (i.e. Garrison, 2006). One example is the ongoing (as of this writing) war in Iraq, which, despite its immediate relevance, appears to be a topic assiduously avoided by many social studies teachers (Davis, 2005; Flinders, 2006).

Constraints of a traditional curriculum. Perhaps the most pressing difficulty, however, is that of responding to unfolding events within the strictures of a chronological, textbook-driven curriculum. Without enduring civic questions and themes to which current events can be anchored, it is difficult to encounter them in any way other than the decontextualized, episodic approach that is typical. The textbook-driven approach to the study of U.S. history drives assessment in many schools, leading to a reduction of U.S. history to a compilation of facts, mainly related to the military and political history of the country. Jill Tenney described how her district's final exam had the potential to narrow instruction, explaining how she resisted this approach:

> The final is all about military history and foreign policy. And Presidential Elections. We covered it, but we didn't spend the majority of our time on it. Because I don't think who ran in 1948 is an important thing to have

and leave the classroom with, as opposed to understanding the arguments behind the immigration issue. To me, anyway. But our school district thinks differently.

The approach featured in this book is designed to facilitate a more meaningful consideration of current events within the curriculum, using current events to enrich the study of history and history to enrich students' understanding of current events.

Approached in this manner, what is current is part of the flow of history. Deep understanding of both is predicated on engagement with larger civic themes. As R. Freedman Butts explained,

> I am, of course, not arguing that U.S. history courses be given over to discussion of the whole range of contemporary issues or current events. Rather, I would argue that there are plenty of current issues that could profitably be approached through fundamental historical study of constitutional principles, especially those that directly affect the rights and obligations of students and teachers under the First, Fifth, and Fourteenth Amendments. And these cannot be adequately understood in isolation from political, social, and cultural history in general.
>
> *(Butts, 1988)*

While this is a compelling and well-articulated vision for how current events might be used as a unifying thread to unite history and the social sciences into a civically meaningful whole, it is difficult to find concrete suggestions for how to achieve this worthy objective within the constraints of current social studies curricula.

Limited best practices. The research literature offers scant suggestions for the meaningful integration of current events into social studies curricula. The Civic Mission of Schools report, as noted earlier, includes "discussion of current issues" as one of the six promising approaches for civic education. While a helpful and significant endorsement of current events teaching, the report offers little in the way of useful guidance for social studies teachers hoping to raise their use of current events beyond the trivial. The authors suggest that teachers should "Incorporate discussion of current local, national, and international issues and events into the classroom, particularly those that young people view as important to their lives." "School administrators," furthermore, "should allow and encourage educators to facilitate discussions of complex and/or controversial current events and issues in the classroom" (Carnegie Corporation and CIRCLE, 2003, p. 7). The closest the authors come to a pedagogical recommendation is to note that student discussion of current events "should be carefully moderated so that students feel welcome to speak from a variety of perspectives" (Carnegie Corporation and CIRCLE, 2003,

p. 6). While an excellent point, this is hardly the stuff upon which to build a new curricular approach to current events instruction.

Other authors provide similar treatment, explaining the sort of experience they wish students to have with current events instruction, while neglecting to provide much in the way of actionable suggestions for curriculum planning. Libresco notes that,

> When I speak of current events instruction, I am not advocating devoting ten minutes on Fridays to the exercise found at the back of the *Weekly Reader* or *Time for Kids* handouts. I mean elementary teachers creating a classroom culture where being informed about world events, and judging and acting in response to them becomes the norm.
>
> *(2002, p. 69)*

Feldman concurs, noting that "Studying current events shouldn't be a 'show and tell' about the events, but a way to expose students to ideas, places, actions and cultures that they might not otherwise know about or understand" (2004, p. 6). Such suggestions do not grapple with the very real difficulties that U.S. history teachers face in trying to create meaningful current connections within the constraints of a textbook-driven curriculum. While this entire book represents an attempt to re-envision the U.S. History curriculum, so as to allow for meaningful integration of civic themes that span past and present, the following section describes three ways that the new curricular and pedagogical approach created by the project team facilitated an approach to current events that was more in line with recommendations on how best to use such instruction to deepen students' civic skills and engagement.

Reframing Current Events for Meaningful Civic Learning

Consideration of current events was an integral part of the new curriculum and central to the design principles upon which the approach was based. Rather than serving as an awkward add-on or a controversial detour, consideration of current world social, economic, and political happenings was built into the design principles and was central to the teachers' beliefs about the purpose of the new curriculum. "My own personal goal is to make social studies more relevant to students' lives," explained Jill. "Ultimately to make it very current," said Bill, reflecting on the purpose of the project.

The project approach. The design principles asserting that civic education should "provide opportunities for students to consider and discuss key issues and controversies in civic life" and "build upon students' own experiences with civic life" ensured that current events would be a fundamental aspect of the project approach.

Essential questions and themes were intentionally selected that could be used to build current events into the very fabric of the curriculum. A question such as "Who is an American?" (from the Movement of People theme), for example, facilitated study and discussion both of turn of the century immigration and current immigration legislation. Within such a framework, SB1070, the 2010 Arizona legislation regarding illegal immigration, could be addressed as part of an ongoing consideration of immigration issues rather than through a one-time engagement destined to shed more heat than light on a complex and controversial topic.

"Current events," proclaimed Kevin Brooks in his final interview, "we did current events all the time." Jill Tenney concurred. When asked when she integrated current events during the project year she responded "all the time." She continued,

> Every day . . . I think that just naturally, through thematic, that was the reason that it was able to be done. Otherwise you'd have to say, "Ok, every Friday we're going to do a current event," if you were teaching chronologically. But because we taught thematically, every day was current events. Because let's say we were talking about immigration. Well, the same problems are happening today that happened 100 years ago, so it's just a matter of pulling that theme through 100 years, and saying, you know, these are the same viewpoints today that people have for and against immigration that they had a hundred years ago. And that's your current event. And you can go on from there and talk about what congress is planning to do on immigration and some of the viewpoints of immigrants and some of the viewpoints of people who are already citizens. We didn't talk about that, but every day, no matter what theme it was, there's always something that relates to the theme that we're doing, and you kind of just pull up and pull through the curriculum.

Both the historical content and the current issues under discussion were enhanced by considering them as part of a whole. Current events instruction was an integral part of the curriculum and pedagogy in all three study schools, although the extent and nature of the instruction varied among the sites.

Box 5.1 shows the design team's initial approach to current events instruction, created during the summer workshop.

In all three schools, current events instruction occurred throughout the year. This section focuses on three overlapping aspects of this integration: connecting current events to history, raising students' understandings of electoral politics and contemporary political issues, and engaging and probing students' perspectives on current events and the civic debates that underlay them. The following examples illustrate both the promise and the complexity of implementing such an approach.

BOX 5.1 GOALS OF CURRENT EVENTS STRAND

Strand 5:

Reading the World—Current Events and Media Literacy in a Problem-Posing Civic Learning Approach

Goals for Students:
- To be able to analyze new stories
- To make connections between selves, world, and curriculum
- To be able to obtain information
- To be able to discern between sources in terms of validity and perspective
- To understand their own avenues for media expression
- To build students' skills of discussion, analysis, critique, and research
- To consider and discuss key issues and controversies in civic life.

Each marking period each class will engage in the following three current events related activities at least once:

1. Teacher-led activity connecting a current event/news story to the curriculum.
2. Students will choose a news event of interest to them, write about it in their social studies journal, and share with the class in some format (pairs, small groups, whole class).
3. Class will engage in an election-related activity drawing on current news events and linked to the curriculum.

Connecting current events to history. Central to the project approach was embedding the study of current events within a greater historical context. Mr. Brooks, as noted in Chapter 2, found that this approach made more sense when trying to get his students to understand historical patterns and cause/effect relationships. "I think it's a lot easier for students to see the cycle," he explained, "how things changed and how they go back and how they change and go back in sort of a pattern." Making these connections helped students to engage with the civic dilemmas underlying the events, both historical and current. "We did current events all year long," Mr. Brooks explained. "We got a lot of mileage out of the Iraq war," he reflected, reminding the interviewer about a lesson in which he discussed the Haditha killings in Iraq in 2005, in which 24 Iraqi men, women, and children were killed by a group of United States Marines, and the My Lai massacre in Vietnam in which a U.S. Army unit killed several hundred unarmed civilians in 1968 during the Vietnam War, with his class, engaging them with the question of what is permissible in war.

Observing an end of semester review for the Conflict and Resolution theme, I watched as Ms. Tenney's student teacher, in February, moved from the Iran hostage crisis to the Iran-Contra affair to Oliver North to the Cold War to the Sandinistas and Contras.

Not only was the class studying more contemporary history in February, they were also considering the big questions and recurring patterns in U.S. conflicts—dilemmas over intervention, humanitarian issues, and national politics.

Jill Tenney described how her student teacher, Kristi, approached the Movement of People theme, embedding current events within the study of U.S. history:

> she did start out with Trail of Tears, and understanding that relocation. Japanese internment. And then Kristi posed the question that after 9/11, some people were calling for some kind of internment or some kind of questioning for Muslim Americans and has the United States changed in 150 years . . .? . . . they talked about immigration by choice, people moving to this country. And they talked about immigration that was happening with Ellis Island in the late 1800s into the early 1900s, and they talked about the Chinese Exclusion Act. And how immigration kind of slowed down a bit in a certain period of time in our country and then picked up again after the 1950s. Different groups of people that came to the United States and why they came and then today, the largest group that comes to the United States, and she talked about our own community . . . our town and how it has changed and why do people come here.

Allwood students, with parents hailing from dozens of countries, easily connected the historical study of immigration with current issues, which will be further explored later.

Mr. Banks also found the theme of immigration to provide a ready opportunity to connect the past to the present in a lesson filled both with valuable connections and missed opportunities. Beginning class with a review of questions that had been assigned for homework, Mr. Banks asked his students "Why has the debate about immigration opened up?" Students offered responses including national security reasons and economic concerns. He moved on to the second question, "Why did the largest group of immigrants come to the U.S.?" This question sparked a detailed explanation of the Irish potato famine and its ensuing impact on immigration in the 19th century.

Mr. Banks briefly explained a few waves of immigration in light of the reading and described the reasons why several groups of immigrants came to the United States. He described the potato famine as being responsible for the wave of Irish immigrants, "economic reasons" for why the Italians came to the U.S., "religious reasons" for Jewish immigration, and "the Chinese came for cheap labor purposes." In discussing the Chinese Exclusion Act of 1882, he told the students how Chinese were banned from coming to the United States. "That's using them," Leticia exclaimed. "That's messed up," Tyronne concurred.

After reviewing the remainder of the homework questions, Mr. Banks transitioned to a series of PowerPoint slides explaining how U.S. citizenship is legally defined. A final slide posed the question "Who deserves citizenship?" He passed out a handout, entitled, "Take-a-Stand: U.S. Citizenship." Students were asked to support or refute the statement on the top of the worksheet that read, "U.S. Citizenship should not be granted, but should be *earned* by *all* citizens." Students first wrote their answers in notebooks and were asked to "prepare to discuss what you've wrote."

Mr. Banks described the "Take-a-Stand Activity." The question generated a lot of interest, with multiple conversations taking place among the students. Chantelle asked for clarification on what it meant to be opposed to granting citizenship. After writing answers in their notebooks, Mr. Banks asked that students stand up to represent their position on the issue. Four students stood on the side of wanting citizenship to be "earned." Seventeen students stood on the other side of the room. "What is a true American?" asked Marcus, but the question went unanswered. After a brief discussion Mr. Banks told his students that they would finish up tomorrow, and class was dismissed.

Students were clearly interested in this activity, both the historical and current aspects of it. They raised questions, including Marcus' close variant of the essential question of the entire year, "What is an American?" The lesson showcases the potential for connecting current events to history and larger civic themes, but also the need to do so with an attentiveness to the key questions underlying both current and historical issues, such as immigration. Bob Banks agreed that essential questions were important. In his first interview he explained,

> the ones we came up with over the summer seem to be giant essential questions, but they are the most important things, really. Where do we come from, what do we stand for, who are we as a people, and where are we going? What are the most important issues, how have they been debated and action been taken over them in the past and then where are we going in the future?

Yet, Bob was also conflicted about reorganizing his curriculum in order to emphasize connections to current issues. He reflected that it "seems like you're losing a lot of the raw history. Which, I don't know, I'm a little conflicted about that." He was uncomfortable with the amount of latitude such an approach gave to students, apprehensive about the potential for class discussions to veer into unplanned territory. The new approach, he explained was meant to "make the classroom less my pulpit and make it their area to discuss," and he found this to be "fairly anxiety inspiring."

Connecting history to the present, as this example illustrates, is more complex than it might seem. Reorganizing the curriculum to highlight places where civic themes undergird historical and current issues opens historical study to interpretation, challenges traditional understandings of who holds and creates knowledge, and unseats the primacy of the textbook as the central vehicle for learning. Such changes, however, have the potential to rejuvenate the social studies classroom, to, as Bob put it, "reinvigorate a dying discipline."

Electoral politics and political issues. In accordance with the strikingly low rate of political awareness among young people described at the outset of this chapter, the project teachers felt their students knew little about current political issues. Kevin described an early activity from the Government theme, saying,

> we looked at the Republicans and a lot of them say, "We hate George Bush," and all sorts of stuff whenever I mention George Bus they're like "ugh," but you start figuring out real quickly that they don't know what's a Republican, and why is a Republican a Republican and why is a Democrat a Democrat?

Jill, contrasting this year, with its direct study of politics through the Government unit, to previous years noted "in years past they wouldn't even know what party Barack Obama and Hillary are from, you know? They would have no idea! 'What's a blue state and what's a red state? Why is this even important?'"

One of the activities in Ms. Tenney's classroom that seemed to make the biggest impression on students was the candidates' forum previously mentioned in Chapter 4. This activity required students to take on the character of a candidate and prepare, through research and writing, to take part in a roundtable discussion on current policy issues, playing the role of that candidate. Jill described,

> with Meet the Candidates I just gave them the requirements and they did all of their own research, and found out where their candidate stood on issues, and they had to write up the briefs so they were prepared for the discussion. They couldn't just print it out from Wikipedia and bring it in to class, everything had to be original. They actually had to read and do some research, and then write in their own words where the candidate stood on issues.

Taking part in the October 2007 candidate forum was an excellent opportunity to showcase the variety of political perspectives on a number of key current issues. Class began with Ms. Tenney explaining the discussion format. She instructed all students to be attentive because in addition to discussing their candidate's positions, they were going to be responsible for writing a reflection paper based on information they heard from other candidates. Each student was to give a one-minute introduction to their candidate, including some biographical information and their reasons for running for the presidency. Candidates represented were Joe Biden, Barack Obama, Chris Dodd, Mike Huckabee, John McCain, Fred Thompson, Alan Keyes, Tom Tancredo, John Edwards, Dennis Kucinich, Bill Richardson, Mike Gravel, Duncan Hunter, Mitt Romney, Sam Brownback, Hillary Clinton, and Ron Paul. The student playing Rudy Giuliani was absent.

Each student had a sheet of talking points in front of them. The first issue that was brought for discussion was the war in Iraq. John Edwards was the first to speak. He spoke about how the Iraq War was a failed foreign policy and that the current strategy was not working. Joe Biden responded in agreement to Edwards. Dennis Kucinich chimed in on the issue of Iraq, declaring that "there is strength in peace." Chris Dodd agreed, saying "it's a waste of taxpayers' money," and "Iraq has made it less safe in America." Bill Richardson said that Iraq has moved us away from what we should be focusing on, which is education. Barack Obama said that we should remove troops from Iraq and begin to open dialogue with Syria and Iran, to which Mike Gravel stated "I agree." Joe Biden put forward that it would be best to "divide Iraq into three regions." Ron Paul mentioned that we went to Iraq with false information and by not declaring war, the war was technically "unconstitutional." Mike Huckabee was the first vocal supporter in the room of the war, saying "the war in Iraq is part of the 'war on terror.'" Hillary Clinton said that Bush misused the authority to go to war. Huckabee quickly responded "if we didn't go to war, there'd be more terrorism."

Ms. Tenney moved the debate from the war in Iraq to healthcare. Mike Gravel opened up the discussion, arguing for universal healthcare. Alan Keyes brought up the Terry Schiavo case, while Edwards supported universal healthcare. Barack Obama said that Americans should have healthcare like the members of Congress have. Ms. Tenney told the students that they would finish up the roundtable on Monday by resuming the discussion and focusing on the issues they did not get to today.

This forum raised a panoply of current issues: healthcare, the war in Iraq, the war on terror, education, and the economy. Through their participation, students learned about the perspectives held by different political parties, political ideology, and the nature of the U.S. national agenda. And, as noted in Chapter 4, such activities develop students' research, writing, and expressive skills.

Student understanding and presentation of policy and history was not always flawless. Ms. Tenney noted,

> There were a few mistakes during the discussion, where they misinterpreted where the candidate stood. But for the most part they were pretty accurate. And then what I did with the students who had the mistakes is I just wrote it down and I just talked to them. You know, by themselves, and said just watch this. You know, but there was, I would say maybe only like three.

> You know like three comments on the wrong side of an issue for a candidate.

While students did not get every detail correct, they used the forum as an opportunity to grapple with the wide variety of perspectives on the numerous issues facing the United States, as well as a chance to reflect on where they themselves stood on these issues.

Directly addressing contemporary political issues and perspectives allowed students to consider current events within the unfolding context of U.S. policy and politics. In the two schools in which teachers implemented the Government theme, Allwood and Surrey, students had the opportunity to cement their knowledge of politics and the political system. Mr. Brooks described his students' deepening understanding of politics, explaining,

> it seems as though my students are trying to see connections between what's happening out there and you know what's happening inside the classroom. I think it's a lot easier for them to see "why is this person Democrat, why do these groups of people vote Democratic, why are Republicans and Democrats not the same, why do these fiscal conservatives tend to vote Republican." I think now they start to get it, where before "these people these Republicans are White people and Democrats are Black and Democrats care about poor people and Republicans are mean they don't care about poor people" that sort of thing and I think they're getting a lot more nuanced in terms of why things are the way they are. I think they definitely know the difference now between criminal and civil law and the different levels of government. I think this way they're learning a lot more. I think that if someone was to ask them a question I think they would be able to answer it and it seems a lot more relevant to them.

Perhaps not the traditional mission of a United States history course, such learning directly addresses the political apathy decried by civic leaders and educators alike.

Exploring students' own perspectives on current issues. The final aspect of the current events approach used by the project team was the way in which the approach allowed students to deeply explore their own perspectives on current issues. Jill Tenney described how her students probed their own feelings about immigration, a deeply personal topic in this diverse, immigrant rich setting,

> they understand the conflicts, they understand how hard it is to become a citizen. And they understand why they come here better than some other students would and when they do discussions on this and structured conversations they brought a lot of their own personal situations and personal viewpoints into the situation. But it was interesting because the immigrants,

the students that are immigrants, who came here legally, were very much opposed to people who came here *ill*egally, and we have both in the classroom. We have illegal immigrants and we have legal immigrants. There's a very, there's almost a resentment among the students who came here legally, and those families that came here legally, versus those who came here illegally. I guess because of how much they had to fight to get here, sacrifice to get here. And people are coming here illegally, and they feel that it's just not fair, I guess.

She described how students directly engaged with each other on this topic, with legal immigrant students saying, "I'm an immigrant, and I came here legally, and I don't think that illegal immigrants should get amnesty or certain benefits and they should go through the process like everyone else," and illegal immigrant students explaining "in my home country, this is the way things are, and we had to get here any way we could and we contribute to the economy, we contribute to the society."

Students felt the power of this personal connection and appreciated the opportunity to express themselves on current issues. Kylie noted that she was most concerned about

the war . . . part of it really bothers me about the whole thing is that they haven't really clarified why we're there. And I mean my brother's friend just got back from Iraq. So I mean thank God he's back and he's safe but I mean I know people that have gone and one of my cousins went . . . we've hit the topic a couple of times when we do, we did these Take-a-Stand things. And those are pretty cool. It gets everyone kind of like talking about like what their own opinions like personal opinions. And that topic came up like are Americans equal? The war in Iraq, all that kind of stuff. Like all fit together.

The topics that were most personally significant to students were those that drew their keenest interest, providing the teachers with ready opportunities to engage students in the sort of engaged civic discussion recommended in the literature.

At Allwood, Take-a-Stands were structured to delve into students' perspectives, as in the following example of a discussion about the Middle East held in February 2008 during the Middle East unit in the Conflict and Resolution theme. Ms. Tenney's student teacher started out the discussion with a statement and students moved to different parts of the room in response.

Teacher: [giving the opening statement] No matter what, I would not be willing to fight in Iraq.

The students split pretty evenly among the two sides.

Winston: I would love to defend my country no matter what, because I love my country. Unless it's like really . . .

Lalit: Like what?

Winston: I don't agree with war in Iraq for economic issues, but I would fight for my country.

Sarah: How many people have lost their legs already for us? If you are willing to sacrifice yourself . . . [then it is a good thing to fight for your country].

Chantelle: I'm not going to go bomb Baghdad. You can be a medic? OK, can I go over there?

She switches from "for" to "against."

Anna: So we're doing this based on a soldier, not a medic or reporter?

Teacher: You could be a nurse.

Ramona: Yeah. [moves from "for" to "against"] I just won't kill anyone. I'd risk my life to save them.

Tamika: I don't approve the war in Iraq, although the point you made yesterday, that if we leave we make ourselves vulnerable, we're over there for no reason at all. But if we are over there for a reason, someone tell me.

Tariq: [standing on "against" side] A lot of you over there, if the draft came up, all of you would be leaving your country.

Samara: You should support the soldiers.

Maria: I'm down with the soldiers.

Marcus: I don't think there is a military way to win the war. There has to be a diplomacy way rather than military. We can't beat them up until they give up.

Noah: [sitting on "against" side] We are talking about people who killed 3000 people! People went to work and didn't come home.

Many voices: That's a different war!

Noah: Same thing. That's why we're over there.

Teacher: 9/11, that's why we invaded Afghanistan. Why did we invade Iraq?

Many voices: Weapons of mass destruction.

Reem: That's none of our business. If someone doesn't like Bush they could come over and attack us?

Tamika: When did they attack us?

Rachel: Maybe they were planning to attack us.

Dan: Don't you want to attack them before they attack us?

Laurie: Saddam Hussein was bad for Iraq. Wasn't he abusing the people?

In this discussion, students are engaging with each other frankly and directly at the sharp edge where current events meet sensitive, personal issues of morality and patriotism. With no abstract discourse, they are getting into questions of where they each draw the line regarding personal sacrifice, harming others, revenge, and the obligation to protect the lives of others, even those not related to us by blood or nationality.

Such discussions could get heated. At one point, Noah exclaimed "Can we just switch topics? This is getting too deep." While the objective of engaging students personally on current events topics is not to upset them, this comment is a clear indication that this lesson went beyond an abstract, surface level consideration of a topic, instead drawing students into a joint consideration of some of the most pressing and pertinent quandaries underlying key civic debates in the United States, both current and past.

Key Conclusions about Integrating Current Events

This exploration of current events instruction in the project classrooms reiterates several earlier themes which I will touch on briefly as I conclude this chapter.

Importance of a thematically organized curriculum. Meaningful current events instruction that furthers the aims of civic learning and engagement is greatly facilitated by the use of a thematically organized curriculum. Such a curriculum allows social studies teachers to move easily between past and present, connecting both to themes that are rich with possibility for discussion, analysis, and personal connection.

Kevin Brooks noted at the end of the year that, because of the thematically organized curriculum,

> I was able to focus a lot more exclusively on contemporary issues than what it was before. Before when I would discuss some things there might have been more just general topics. But now I can specifically bring in more current things they might be familiar with.

Jill Tenney explained that "everything, every theme, lent itself, and every unit within the theme, lent itself to talk about a current event." Themes helped to move the study of current events beyond an episodic approach that trivialized them. By connecting current events directly to the ongoing curriculum, they became part of the regular course of study, enriched by and enriching students' study of history.

Importance of essential questions. Open-ended essential questions were critical for connecting current events study to underlying civic issues and debates. Such questions help teachers realize the often untapped civic learning potential of student study of current and historic events. Questions such as "When should the U.S. go to war?", "What do Americans owe each other?" and "Who is an American?" are open to debate and can be illuminated by examination of both historic and contemporary affairs. Equally useful in inciting discussion of both past and present events, such questions catapult students right into the midst of ongoing civic debates, putting history into motion and uncovering the civic quandaries at the heart of social studies.

Difficulties of using current events for meaningful civic learning within a chronological approach. A chronological approach, on the other hand, seems to thwart the meaningful use of current events. Bob Banks described his approach to current events in his chronological curriculum as happening "as things came up," explaining that,

> Every once in a while I'd throw it into a sort of a do-now or there was one time when we were just talking about Jim Crow laws and then I handed them a Jena Six article about that. And we had a discussion based on it. But . . . I'm not sure that I did current events where it would really fit into our, the curriculum that was drawn.

In the end, he was faced with a frustration common to social studies teachers: not being able to "get to today." He felt he did not have "enough time. In terms of the regular curriculum, I didn't get much past 1977."

He put the blame on the chronologically organized curriculum, saying,

> teaching the curriculum in a chronological manner like this district does, like this department does, it's such a time suck that I was really, really disappointed that I didn't get past Jimmy Carter. So disappointed. I swore to myself at the beginning of this year I'm going to get to Clinton and it just didn't happen.

This was not an exceptional year. When I asked if he would usually "get to Clinton," he responded "Never. And I was like this is going to be the first time." He was upset about this, reflecting "it's so frustrating because these kids, a lot of them were born in 1991 and they didn't learn anything about the Gulf War and it makes me sad."

In the end, what appears to be perhaps the most common-sense and simple aspect of social studies teaching, current events instruction, might necessitate dramatic curricular reorganization if U.S. history teachers wish to maximize the civic learning potential of contemporary affairs. As this chapter illustrates, current events instruction can be transformed into a powerful aspect of an approach to U.S. history that puts meaningful civic learning at the center.

6

WHAT'S THE PROBLEM?

Civic Action Research in the Social Studies Classroom[1]

I've never really had to like think [inaudible] on like a certain topic . . . it was interesting finding out about the school and being able to go out and get to know the school better and talking to teachers about it. It was just really fun.

(Percy, Oak Knoll High School)

We've never done anything like this before in school.

(Tamika, Surrey High School)

It was something we all wanted to do. It was a problem we all wanted to do, so everyone got involved. It felt good because we got to make change.

(Samara, Allwood High School)

In 2003/2004, Brian Schultz engaged his fifth grade class, students at a public elementary school in a low-income Chicago neighborhood, in a year-long project in which they took on a deeply felt issue—investigating and documenting the poor condition of their dilapidated school building and advocating for a new school. Working collaboratively, Schultz's students investigated, marshaled resources, and presented their research in a variety of formats including presentations to local school and government officials, newspaper articles, radio shows, and a book authored by Schultz (Schultz, 2008). While the students did not achieve their desired goal of a new school, they engaged in authentic and meaningful learning that integrated literacy, social studies, statistics, and civics throughout the year.

---

1   This chapter draws in part on previously published work: Rubin & Jones, 2007; Rubin, Hayes, & Benson, 2009; and Rubin & Hayes, 2010.

Research indicates that engaging students in discussion, investigation, and analysis of the civic problems they encounter in their daily lives holds potential for fostering more aware and empowered civic identities (Fine et al. 2007; Hess, 2009; Kahne & Westheimer, 2003; Rubin, 2007; Rubin & Hayes, 2010). Youth action research, with its emphasis on involving students in meaningful inquiry on self-generated topics linked to their own lives and experiences, is a potential antidote to the rote approaches that dominate civic education in many settings, particularly in schools serving low-income students (Kahne & Middaugh, 2008). There are many examples of how educational experiences that foster sociopolitical development and critical inquiry can contribute to the civic empowerment of youth from marginalized communities (e.g. Abu El-Haj, 2009b; Morrell, 2004; Watts, Griffith, & Abdul-Adil, 1999).

Student action research has strong civic education possibilities, and has been used as such, with empowering results for students, by a number of educational researchers working in an anthropological tradition (e.g. Berg, 2004; Cammarota & Romero, 2009; Stoudt, 2009). Despite the potential of civic action research to make the social studies curriculum more relevant, meaningful, and rich with opportunity for the development of key civic competencies, civic action research has yet to permeate social studies instruction, long considered to be the primary site for civic education.

In this chapter, I consider the possibilities of adapting youth civic action research for the social studies classroom. I describe the disparate traditions that the project team drew upon to develop its approach to integrating a civic action research strand into the curriculum, depict the twists and turns of these efforts at the three study schools, and outline the dilemmas and rewards of implementing such projects.

Youth Action Research for Civic Learning

Student action research—projects conducted by youth to inform and impact problems they see around them—has proliferated in recent years both nationally and internationally. Going by various names—participatory research, action research, participatory evaluation—student action research is research that: 1) is conducted by youth, within or outside of schools and classrooms, with the goal of informing and impacting school, community and/or global problems and issues, and 2) contributes to the positive development of a variety of academic, social, and civic skills in youth (Park, 1993; Sabo, 2003). Many, although not all, youth-led, participatory research and evaluation projects share a social activist stance (Powers & Tiffany, 2006). At its best, student action research engages youth, particularly underrepresented and disadvantaged youth, in critical exploration of issues that impact their lives inside and outside of school (Rubin & Jones, 2007).

This project brought together several interrelated, yet distinct approaches to conducting inquiry projects with youth that I will describe in detail below. Youth participatory action research (YPAR) emphasizes youth empowerment and is rooted in a critical analysis of race, class, and power. Project Citizen, a federally funded curriculum effort, is embedded in a neo-liberal, policy-driven approach that focuses on citizenship skills. The project also drew upon the long tradition, rooted in progressive educational philosophies, of inquiry-driven instruction in the social studies.

The Youth Participatory Action Research Approach

In New York City, a diverse group of youth surveyed thousands of their peers about their experiences related to race, integration, segregation, and the "opportunity gap" in their schools, producing a DVD of spoken word performances that drew upon this data (Torre, 2009). In a refugee camp in Kenya, a team of 11 young people investigated the experiences of youth in the camps, conducting over 140 interviews and focus groups, meeting several times a week to map emerging themes, and eventually producing a final report and a public presentation for audiences of refugee youth in another camp, camp staff, and the leadership of other NGOs (Cooper, 2005). In another project, young people used photography to investigate community issues, creating an exhibit on violence in their community (McIntyre, 2000). Research in the youth participatory action research (YPAR) tradition is built upon such critical analyses of social inequalities, along with a critique of traditional modes of research and commitment to incorporating youth as co-researchers, not just as a means of developing their skills and engagement but to add underrepresented and hidden knowledge to the research base.

Building on the emancipatory educational theory of Paulo Freire, participatory action research aims to empower and liberate through the process of participant-led inquiry. The cornerstone of this approach is that participants take part in conducting research on the issues that impact them directly. Wadsworth writes,

> [Participatory action research is] research which involves all relevant parties in actively examining together current action (which they experience as problematic) in order to change and improve it. They do this by critically reflecting on the historical, political, cultural, economic, geographic and other contexts which make sense of it.
>
> *(Wadsworth, 1998)*

These projects most often take place outside of the constraints of the classroom as part of after-school or community programs (e.g. Cahill, 2007; Tuck, 2009); they are less frequently integrated into classroom curricula (e.g. Berg, 2004; Cammarota & Romero, 2009). They can be run by scholars (e.g. Torre, 2009), community organizations (e.g. Owens & Jones, 2004; Schensul, LoBianco, & Lombardo, 2004) or even global nongovernmental organizations (NGOs) such as UNICEF (e.g. Maglajlic et al., 2004). Students study a variety of self-selected issues, including bullying and school violence (e.g. Stoudt, 2009), the test score gap between students of color and White students (e.g. Torre, 2009), the stereotyping of youth of color (e.g. Cahill, 2007), gaps in support for LGBTQ (lesbian, gay, bisexual, transgender and queer) youth (e.g. Owens & Jones, 2004), youth violence (e.g. Bingham & Christie, 2004), and school conditions (e.g. Schultz, 2008).

YPAR projects emphasize youth choice, a democratic approach to relationships among adults and youth involved with the project, critical analysis, and a commitment to research as a form of empowerment. The *Participatory Action Research Curriculum for Empowering Youth* produced by the Institute for Community Research (ICR, 2004) describes participatory action research as:

> an inquiry process that includes critical and creative thinking and communications skills, raising questions and discovering answers in a group, analysis skills and problem solving for action. At the same time, because it is a group activity, PAR builds interpersonal relationships, and strengthens individual and group capacity for social action. Youth PAR empowers youth as individuals by building skill sets. It empowers them as a group in learning and acting together. It empowers them socially by supporting them to work for social justice and social change.
>
> *(p. 7)*

A critical take on social inequality is fundamental to YPAR projects. The ICR curriculum guide, for example, grounds its approach in critical theory, which it describes as follows:

> Inequities in class, power, racial/ethnic status, and educational quality and individual achievement, and access to political power are embedded in institutions that have power over peoples' lives (public institutions, national and local policies, service agencies, workplaces and policing agencies). It is very important to understand both the specifics of the inequities, and the ways that they are supported by these institutions. At the same time, to bring about change (to reduce or eliminate inequities), it is necessary to reflect on one's personal position and personal responsibility to change. Once these are understood, people are able to act to transform themselves and oppressive institutions, and to reduce or eliminate social inequities.
>
> *(pp. 9–10)*

Empowerment, another key element, is described as:

> the ability of an individual to make decisions that change their own lives. In this context, resistance means withstanding pressures to behave in undesired and undesirable ways . . . Collective empowerment also means the ability of a group to work toward bringing about transformative social change, that is

to change the institutions that promote social injustice, that create and support the unequal distribution of financial, social and political resources and access to power . . .

(p. 10)

Thus, YPAR projects are embedded in a vision of youth research that is emancipatory and critical.

Beyond the philosophical framing of YPAR projects, these endeavors focus on engaging youth in substantial original research using both traditional and innovative methodologies. Students learn how to develop, conduct, and analyze the results of surveys, interviews, and focus groups. They often use nontraditional data collection strategies as well, including photography, mapping, journaling, and distributing "slam books" (collaboratively written journals) to peers. Student findings are shared through a variety of formats, from a more traditional oral presentation of research to photo exhibits, protests, videos, spoken work performances, skits, and scrapbooks.

The project team appreciated the way that the YPAR approach roots research problems in students' experiences, aims to empower youth through the development of research and analytical skills, and takes a critical perspective on the inequalities some youth face in their daily lives. We drew upon other inquiry traditions as well.

The Project Citizen Approach

The project also drew upon more traditional, civic education-oriented approaches to youth action research. The most well-developed and widespread example of these is the Project Citizen curriculum developed and disseminated by the federally funded Center for Civic Education. The Project Citizen curriculum, first implemented in 1995, is based on the notion that engaging young people in active investigation of youth-selected problems and development of policy solutions will increase their civic knowledge, dispositions, and skills. It features public policy analysis, cooperative learning, and a problem-solving methodology that hearkens back to Dewey (Atherton, 2000). As of Fall 2008, approximately 32,200 teachers have used the curriculum, with almost two million students taking part. The curriculum has been translated into more than 40 languages and is used around the world.

Whereas YPAR projects focus on youth empowerment through an investigation of a self-selected problem, "the primary goal of Project Citizen," as stated in an overview,

is to develop in students a commitment to active citizenship and governance by: providing the knowledge and skills required for effective citizenship, providing practical experience designed to foster a sense of competence and efficacy, developing an understanding of the importance of citizen participation.

(Center for Civic Education, 2009, Slide 3)

The objectives of encouraging specific citizenship skills are central to Project Citizen. As an outside research organization hired to assess the curriculum and its implementation describes it, Project Citizen's "primary aim is to teach students in Grade 5–12 how to monitor and influence public policy in the context of a specific community problem" (Root & Northup, 2007, p. i).

Project Citizen walks students through the selection of a community problem that can be addressed by public policy. Students identify public policy problems in their communities, conduct preliminary research on a number of problems, select a problem for class study, gather information on the problem, and develop a class portfolio that explains the problem, evaluates alternative policies, and proposes a constitutionally consistent policy proposal and an action plan for getting the policy implemented. Many Project Citizen classes participate in local, state, and even national Project Citizen showcases in which students present their portfolios to panels of judges.

Project Citizen provides teachers and students with a formal structure for uncovering and addressing civic problems, with a focus on finding policy solutions for local civic issues. Independent evaluators have found that students who participated in Project Citizen increased their knowledge of public policy and democracy, improved their persuasive writing and civic discourse skills, and improved their public policy and problem-solving skills as well as their ability to articulate, research, and advocate policy solutions in written form (Roots & Northup, 2007).

Despite differences in ideological framing, both YPAR and Project Citizen share a commitment to youth investigation of youth-generated problems as a means to personal, political, and civic empowerment. The Project Citizen curriculum does not involve as extensive data collection and analysis efforts as do most YPAR projects; YPAR projects are not necessarily aimed at public policy solutions. The distinctions between these two approaches may not matter much to young people in the end, as the research experience is fairly similar. Indeed, Brian Schultz's students' project, described at the outset of this chapter, began as a Project Citizen assignment, but blossomed into something more akin to YPAR. In our project, we wanted to preserve the careful scaffolding and civic orientation of the Project Citizen approach while allowing students to engage with issues related to inequality and personal experience and develop research skills, as is more typical of YPAR.

Inquiry and Active Learning in Progressive Education

Both YPAR and Project Citizen draw upon the long tradition of student inquiry and active participation in learning that are cornerstones of progressive approaches to education. John Dewey wrote in 1938,

> There is, I think, no point in the philosophy of progressive education which is sounder than its emphasis upon the importance of the participation of the learner in the formation of the purposes which direct his activities in the learning process.
>
> *(Dewey, 1938, p. 77)*

Progressive educational philosophy centers on the notion of active student participation in the learning process, concepts at the heart of both YPAR and Project Citizen. Kaplan notes that "phrases like 'learning by doing,' 'democracy in action,' and 'creating a caring community of learners,'" fundamental precepts of civic action research projects of all stripes, "are based on Dewey's teachings" (Kaplan, 2002, p. 158).

Civic Action Research in the Study Schools

During the summer workshop, the project team read about and discussed examples of youth participatory action research projects, grappling with the idea that meaningful civic learning should have a research and action component. The project team decided that a civic action research strand would be a powerful addition to the curricular reform. As Jill Tenney reflected, this strand could embody all of the design principles:

> I think they all link [all of the design principles to civic action research]. The students get to choose the problems, it's their own experiences. It gives them opportunities to consider key issues in their community . . . I think it gives them the power to understand that they have a voice. Even though they can't vote . . . they can enter the conversation, "I can have an opinion now, I can influence others."

Civic action research aligned perfectly with the design principles, embodying the notion that students should use their own civic experiences as a means for the development of important civic skills.

Kevin Brooks was passionate about the need for a strand that would tie the curriculum directly to action. As he reflected,

> my goal is still the same I want them to actually see that they can do things to make a difference somehow . . . I want them to develop the sense of caring enough like "this is my city I live here this is my country" . . . something as

small as recognizing that this is their block, this is their neighborhood, this is their school, and when there is something that actually needs change and I can actually do something to change things towards things I think that are better . . . so many people don't really get the sense that they can actually do something. They really feel powerless . . . because they don't really know how to grasp with something that they'd like to change . . . So I want to kind of push them along where they can actually see things that they're able to do.

For Mr. Brooks, it was critical that his students begin to think of themselves as a part of a larger community, with the power to make a difference on things that mattered to them.

With these ideas in mind, the team agreed upon goals for the civic action research strand, depicted in Box 6.1.

Each school had its own experience with the civic action research strand, with distinct challenges, dilemmas and accomplishments. The next section will describe the twists and turns of the civic action research implementation at each school.

BOX 6.1 GOALS OF CIVIC ACTION RESEARCH STRAND

Strand 3:

Civic Action Research

Students will take part in a civic action research project throughout the year. Students can work in groups or as a class, whichever best meets the needs of the students and teacher.

Goals for Students:
- To have community knowledge
- To act in the world
- To get outside the classroom
- To engage with community issues of concern to them
- To come up with suggestions/solutions for a civic problem
- To learn how to make change
- To learn to gather data/information
- To be heard (present their results to others)
- To build upon students' own experiences with civic life, including daily experiences with civic institutions and their agents
- To build students' discussion, analysis, critique, and research skills
- To build students' knowledge of their rights and responsibilities as citizens in a way that connects directly to their own concerns.

The Allwood Experience: School-Based Problem Resolved with Little Effort

At Allwood High School, the civic action research strand began with great excitement as students presented and discussed potential problems they could investigate. Groups of students took turns presenting their ideas for civic problems and the results of their initial research to one another.

> "We should have the same stuff as Underwood" [the district's other high school].
> "Battle of the Bands!"
> "Pep rallies!"
> "If we have more activities, when we get compared to Underwood we'll look better."
> "Hasn't anyone noticed it has gotten progressively worse every year, they are taking more and more away from us?"
> "Yeah!"

Boisterous with overlapping voices, the room filled with students' ideas and questions. The tone was giddy and impassioned, students interjecting, questioning, and voicing agreement. Hands waved around the room, as students asked each other questions, raised issues, made comments, added examples, and focused intently on the identification and discussion of problems they had selected for consideration—the dress code, crowded conditions at lunch, the difficulty getting through halls during passing periods, and the rule against carrying backpacks through the halls.

A student named Raman described to us some of the problems they discussed during the selection process:

> We said lunches, how they should be longer. And how they should have better food for us . . . we also talked about during passing [from class to class], how we should have more time . . . because it's hard to, like, get around because it's so crowded . . . to get to the other class on time.

Students were frustrated with the stance the school administration took toward them ("They're so strict!" a girl exclaimed about the dress code). Robbie explained, "the way they, the way the teachers treat kids, and the administration, it's like the rules are so ridiculous that they encourage people to break them."

Ms. Tenney had been trained to use the Project Citizen curriculum and had implemented it previously. She was comfortable with the process of brainstorming problems with her students and helping them to narrow down their choices and consider the pros and cons of selecting each problem. She encouraged her students to brainstorm widely, which they did, coming up with such problems as discrimination in which religious holidays are observed on the school calendar, dress code, the rule against backpacks in the hallway, cafeteria food quality, school policies about pep rallies, and more. Student groups conducted preliminary research on these issues and made presentations to each other.

Ms. Tenney confirmed that in recent years the school administration had developed additional rules, increasingly restricting and regulating students' school lives. Students were growing frustrated. The administration's response to student infractions over the past few years had been to take away privileges in the name of curbing disorderly conduct: pep rallies, the ability to wear backpacks, field trips, and more. The extremely crowded state of the school, which currently handled many more students than it had been designed to accommodate, exacerbated these problems and spurred multiple difficulties (e.g., the length of lunch, packed hallways). Students thought that wearing backpacks, so they would not have to go to their lockers between classes, might alleviate some of these issues.

For this reason, Ms. Tenney's classes decided to investigate and act upon the rule against wearing backpacks in the hallways. This problem coincided with a transition in school leadership; a new principal replaced the principal who had implemented the backpack rule, and Ms. Tenney had the students hold back on their project as they waited to see how the new administrator would approach school policy. As the year progressed, Ms. Tenney, as the most faithful adherent to the newly designed curriculum, had her hands full with the new activities and projects it entailed. Students enthusiastically participated in the many class discussions and the expressive projects described earlier, limiting the time she had available for the action research project and buttressing her decision to hold off on proceeding with the project until they saw what the new leader would do. By the third quarter, the quarter in which students were going to focus on developing a policy plan to address their problem, the new principal eliminated the backpack rule, allowing students to wear cloth backpacks that closed with drawstrings as they walked through the school hallways.

Despite the way in which the problem they had selected had been resolved, Ms. Tenney's students felt that their civic action project work had been successful. Tariq described the events proudly,

> We picked the backpack situation, [which] actually got done. We didn't even have to do anything. It just got done because of the new principal. Because I think he realized how nonsense that was. Not to have backpacks. So what he did was he let us have string bags. Little sport bags. So we really, we won the battle.

Samara, quoted at the beginning of the chapter, explained,

> it was something we all wanted to do. It was a problem we all wanted to do so everyone got involved . . . Last year there was a lot of threats and stuff,

and the principal didn't want us to carry around backpacks. So that was our problem—trying to, like, get the principal to let us use our backpacks . . . It felt good because we got to make change. Like, now we can carry backpacks.

Students even felt they had had an impact on resolving some of the problems that they had not selected to address. Lalit discussed how the principal had lengthened the passing time allowed between class periods, one of the problems students had considered but had not chosen for further study. "I don't know if our class really affected it much," he conceded, "but we do have more passing time next year. Yeah, so I don't think it was our class specifically, but I think we did make a difference."

Reflecting on the year, Ms. Tenney felt that the civic action research strand was the most challenging aspect of the entire curricular redesign for her. It was "the most difficult to implement because of the change in administration, the change of attitude in the school . . . by dealing with a school problem, and then with change in administration, every single class's problem was addressed throughout the school year." She felt that by selecting a school-based problem, the students limited the significance of the project, reflecting "it should have been a community problem instead of a school problem." However her students had difficulty finding a community problem about which they could all feel passionately. As noted in Chapter 1, Allwood had a relatively high median income (over $80,000 per family), low percentages of families living in poverty (2.7%), and low unemployment (4.2%) and violent crime (1.6%) rates. Ms. Tenney linked her students' difficulties finding a broad community problem to the fairly sheltered nature of their lives in the middle class, bedroom suburb of Allwood:

> with the community problem, it's so hard in a town of our size, and because we are a middle-class suburb, to really find a problem that's meaningful to all students. Because, I mean, it's, there are problems out there, but I don't know how passionate the students are about some of the problems that the community has . . . I'm not sure how they would choose a problem and be passionate enough about it. I mean what their hardest thing that they have to deal with, traffic?

She still felt the strand was "valuable," but wanted to consider how to improve its implementation for Allwood students. For students, the civic action strand at Allwood was eclipsed by other aspects of the curriculum, although they ended the year feeling like they had made a difference through their somewhat truncated study of school-based civic problems.

The Oak Knoll Experience: A New Approach for Teacher and Students

In Oak Knoll, Bob Banks was curious about what problems his students might come up with. His students were racially and socioeconomically diverse, therefore, he wondered what sort of topic for investigation they might agree upon. At the beginning of the year, he reflected,

> I will be interested to see what my kids come up with because there's the whole "up the hill, down the hill" [affluent and low income students separated geographically] thing. I got kids sitting in there that live in gated communities and I got kids that, you know, live with their extended families in a roach infested apartment. So . . . I'll be very interested to see where they come together on this.

This proved to be an astute observation about the possible complications of a project rooted in students' daily lives and experiences.

Having never led students through a similar project, Mr. Banks did not have the same comfort level as did Ms. Tenney with the notion of youth action research. He was unfamiliar with the process of research and expressed discomfort about leading this aspect of the project. He described his hesitations, saying,

> Um, just in terms of action research, literally teaching them how to research. And, you know, how, for me to, to be able to go out and seek out what the community resources are. And then to find some way to find the time, and the proper structure in order to lead them to that.

He was concerned about the time the project might take away from the rest of his curriculum as well as his students' willingness and ability to dedicate their time after school hours. He noted,

> And the simple fact that, these are kids, that most of them have jobs, you know, most of them are in extracurricular activities. If it is something of this scope, where do they find the time? How much time am I able to give them in order to get this done?

A project based on student interest and investigation that could take many possible routes was an unfamiliar practice for Mr. Banks. Perhaps for this reason, the project seemed like an add-on to him, rather than an integrated part of his curriculum, and he was concerned about fitting it into the rest of the year.

Mr. Banks wanted his students to be personally invested in the project, so he did not require the class to select one problem. "To me that seems *patently* unfair because that's not necessarily what you're most interested in," he reflected.

Students, working in small groups and pairs, selected various problems to work on, including the condition of the school building, lack of after-school activities for youth in Oak Knoll, town taxes, poor drivers and driving conditions, racial profiling, student self-segregation, teen unemployment, police harassment of teens, and school start time. While admirable, this meant that the students skipped the step of conducting preliminary research on a variety of topics, presenting on and debating the merits of these problems, and coming together as a class on one issue that was significant to all of them. It also meant that Mr. Banks needed to support students as they used various means to investigate a disparate set of problems, with the potential for each to entail a distinct action plan and final product.

As each group worked to research their own problem, some of the groups became bogged down in problems typical of group work in a setting in which collaborative learning is an anomaly; progress was impeded by student absences and poorly functioning groups. Perhaps in response, Mr. Banks became more focused on the product that his students were to produce, coming up with a menu of options (e.g. flyer, PowerPoint presentation, letter). He reported that students were generally unenthusiastic about this aspect of the project. In the end, he felt the students had been invested in their chosen problems, but he was disappointed in the products they produced.

> At least we got them to try and think about their community. At the very least, we got them to work somewhat cooperatively in a group and to get excited about the fact that it was their choice. Oh OK, this is what I care about OK. We hit a brick wall when it comes to actually thinking about how to implement solutions. That was I'm not sure why but it was near impossible for most of the kids to take even the tiniest next step to "here's what I found out and here's what the problem is and then OK. What can be done about it? I'm just a kid. I have no power. Nobody's going to listen to me. Oh it's just a problem, it's always existed and I can't fix it."

He felt the students were limited in their ability to imagine and present solutions to the problems they had investigated and reflected a sense of powerlessness rather than civic efficacy.

The students, however, enthusiastically described how they had investigated and attempted to act upon the problems they had selected. Ernie explained how his group tackled poor maintenance of school facilities:

> we see ceilings falling, well I haven't seen, but they've seen rats . . . I've seen stuff like leaky ceilings, and water coming out . . . we were doing percentages and trying to get students' opinions. We did surveys. And then we went to Oak Knoll online and saw their budget. We were trying to see if they're financially good. And we found out a lot of things, like the school budget, the ranking of schools . . . they wasted a lot of money on the fields

. . . We wrote two letters. I wrote it to the mayor and another person wrote it for the Board of Education. And we wrote the statistics and the students' opinions and we put the percentages into the essay.

Had he ever done anything like this project before? "No." Did he feel that he had accomplished something?

I thought it was helpful. Because even though it was a project, I still felt like . . . this is partially something you can do to change the community and to give your opinion out. And I felt like this is pretty easy and it's effective. Like just writing your opinion down and giving it to the Board of Education.

Emma, whose group had investigated police harassment of youth, described how:

we did research in the county and also we tried to research in Oak Knoll. And go around and do surveys in Oak Knoll and give them to people from adults to kids. And ask them questions, if they have been, if they haven't been, if they know someone that has been, and how do you feel about the situation. And a good percent had been.

Their group produced a flyer titled "Racial Profiling in Oak Knoll," which contained a descriptive article, "Is it more of a problem than we thought?", the results of their survey on racial profiling ("Have you experienced racism personally? 49%—yes; 51%—no and When you enter certain establishments, do you feel you are being watched based on your physical appearance, race or color? 65%—yes; 35%—no"), and a data table of stops, searches and arrests categorized by racial group in Oak Knoll. The flyer also describes a program to end racial profiling that was instituted in Ontario and suggests Oak Knoll adopt it. This student group's results were surprising to Mr. Banks. "I learned that they get hassled out in the real world more than I thought they would," he reflected. "By police officers, by authority figures. Two different groups did police harassment and racial profiling. I was like, 'really?'"

Percy explained how his group had investigated school spending and created a video presentation.

We found the budget of the school. Got a whole bunch of information from different teachers, people who were working here for a long time . . . From vice principals to custodians . . . we actually got new teachers and asked them about the school that they came from . . . So we asked a whole bunch of students questions too. It's a video . . . like a presentation with clips on each slide.

Amaya explained her group's project on teen employment:

> my project that I'm doing is teen employment and I wrote a letter to the
> co-op advisor, so maybe they can get more people to open up their jobs,
> especially during the summertime, or you know, have more career-based
> jobs . . . If you can start a committee that helps kids who are serious about
> getting a high-paying job . . . That's what I wrote in my letter.

Her group produced a flyer with graphs showing employment rates and types
of employment for teens. Quincy, a student who had bounced around between
different high schools in the region, explained how his group had gathered data
on their problem, the lack of after-school activities for high school aged students.

> We surveyed what kind of after school activities would most teenagers want
> . . . A lot of people they'd like more basketball, of course, football, stuff like
> that . . . And then we did a survey on what people do now, as there's no
> activities right now. They just stay home, some people just stay home, play
> video games, go to other places.

His group's flyer describes the results of their survey of 200 students,
concluding,

> In our opinion, we feel that if students had activities to do after school there
> would be less crime and less of a chance of anything bad happening to them.
> A shocking 98% of the students interviewed believe that with more activities
> closer to them, there would be less illegal activities, such as drug distribution
> and using.

Zev described how his group had investigated the impact of an early school
starting time and advocated for change saying,

> we went online and looked at the disorders or illnesses caused by lack of
> sleep. Anxiety, restlessness, insomnia, stuff like that . . . how kids during the
> day are like they just always complain "I'm so tired, I'm so tired." That could
> dramatically affect the test scores. So we thought that if school was pushed
> back and people got more rest and time to eat food in the morning maybe
> test scores would go up. Moods would be better, less fight. It would just
> make everything run smoothly . . . We did petitions. We sent emails out to
> Board of Ed members, the principal. We interviewed the principal about
> what he thought about this. We interviewed some parents . . .

Student after student described their work on the project and, to a one, said
that they had never done anything like this civic action research project before in
school.

The Surrey Experience: Scrapbook Journey Through Difficult Problems

At the third school, the project took yet another turn. Starting with community problems, Kevin Brooks' students trended in the opposite direction from Ms. Tenney's, choosing complex, irresolvable community problems: drugs and murder. Mr. Brooks explained to the project team:

> so they choose drugs and my second period class choose murders . . . Which you know is rough but you and I was trying to put any, any, any barriers on what they what they wanted to do you know I mean it's a civic driven uh civic participation driven uh program . . . I really didn't want them to feel like this is a typical school thing . . .

Mr. Brooks described how his class arrived at these problems:

> What I did was I had them set up a chart where they pretty much, they're thinking about their block, their neighborhood, their city and the school— places where you spend most of your time . . . So [I asked] what do you like about them, what do you hate about them . . . I said "draw from the things that you hate and pick what you'd like to change."

"Uniforms and lunches were things that they hated," Mr. Brooks told us, problems shared by Allwood students. But, in the end, his students decided to tackle a community problem very different from Allwood's. Manuel described how the students in his class made their choice, selecting "drugs" after honing it down to "drugs" and "murder," because the former was tightly linked to the latter. He explained, "Because, it's basically like, if we would of chose murder, most of the murders here in Surrey are dealt with drugs, so basically if you stop drugs . . . you're stopping most of the murders."

Mr. Brooks recognized the seriousness of the problems his students had selected. They reflected students' experiences of the high violent crime rate (22.8%), low median family income ($23,000), high unemployment rate (16%), and high percentage of families living in poverty (over 48%), noted in Chapter 1. The topics were "rough" he said, acknowledging the difficulty of doing projects on such choices.

Beyond the obvious seriousness and intractability of the problems the students had selected to investigate, Mr. Brooks explained that the involvement of some of his students in the very problems they had chosen to investigate made the project still more complex. "I mean I understand the make-up of my students," he said. "I mean I have some people that just left jail, I got quite a few students that have these behavioral programs, that are drug dealers themselves, that are drug dealers right now." The students had considered examining teenage pregnancy, an all-too-common occurrence in Surrey, but had instead chosen drugs as they saw that problem at the root of the other issues of violence in the community. Yet, Mr. Brooks continued, laughing wryly, "in a way that's going to be kind of awkward. I mean you got some people that are selling drugs that are going to find a way to tackle drugs as an issue."

He was hopeful and committed to the project as a means of empowering his students as citizens and indeed as people,

> actually to let them know that you're able to fight for things and you're able to bring attention to things. I think that's a big thing. That's why I really hope that this . . . I really would like to have a rally I would like to do things I would like to really play it up where I'm calling people, I'm calling the newspaper . . . so they can actually see themselves in the newspaper fighting for something . . . and I'll do whatever I can to help make that sort of thing come to pass. I mean I really want them to see that they're being spotlighted for something positive and for trying to change something which I don't think they've experienced just yet . . . you know I mean these kids get yelled at all day I mean they curse in class they get fussed at all the time . . . but now actually a lot of attention is being brought to them doing something positive maybe that carries on . . .

In this vein, he encouraged his students to take part in community events, requiring them to attend school board and town council meetings and stay abreast of community news.

Mr. Brooks' students were highly motivated to make a difference in their community. Manuel wrote in his journal:

> My plan after high school is to go to the Air Force for about four years. After I finish the Air Force, I want to go to the police academy so I can help stop the drugs in Surrey. So, the kids in the future won't have to go through what I went through.

He wanted to change things for younger children:

> I don't really talk for myself, because I can handle my, I can work, you know? I really talk for the younger people. My brother, I want things better for my brother. I don't want to see my younger brother go on a bad path. So I don't really talk for me, I'm already 18; I'm ready to hit the real world. You know. I'm talking for the younger kids that got talent, that actually want to be somebody.

Yet, despite their desire to help, many students expressed discouragement and hopelessness based on the situations they faced. In interviews and class discussions, students described solutions as elusive, beyond their control, and personally dangerous.

The quandary of civic action in this setting was on full display during a class discussion in the midst of the Conflict and Resolution theme. What follows is an excerpt from a discussion, led by Mr. Brooks, on the Edmund Burke quote "The only thing necessary for the triumph of evil is for good men to do nothing."

Mr. Brooks: If I asked you that, what do you think it [the quote] means? For evil to happen, good people must sit back and do nothing.
Manuel: It's true. Yes, there's a lot in this community that you see that you can't do something about—drugs.
Mr. Brooks: Suppose you thought something was right—is it always right to get involved?
Evan: You know drugs are bad but you can't fix it.
Mr. Brooks: What about drug dealers . . . you see them in the same spot, same day, all the time . . . What if you were to report them?
Manuel: You can't snitch in the hood. You get popped.

What for those living in more affluent communities might seem to be an obvious action, calling the police to report drug dealing, for Surrey students, would involve great personal risk. Students frequently encountered what they knew to be dangerous and illegal activity, without feeling as if they could do anything about it. Manuel reflected this sense of hopelessness, saying, "One person can't make a difference. If it's one don't get involved." "I can't do anything where I live," echoed Evan. Narciso wavered a bit, telling the interviewer "if a lot of people get together, they could like stop it [drug dealing] a little bit," before concluding, "but it ain't never going to stop."

Faced with the difficulties of addressing these complex problems coupled with his students' sometimes inconsistent school attendance and general academic struggles, Mr. Brooks devised an approach to the civic action research project that was both process and product, a "scrapbook" of students' research and personal reflections on drugs and violence in their communities. The scrapbook was flexible enough to accommodate the shifting population in Mr. Brooks' classrooms, provided space for different kinds of writing, helped students improve little-used skills, and provided a tangible outcome for their work. A means for students to document the various ways in which their lives had been impacted by murder and drugs, the scrapbook motivated students to write for an audience of school, community, and state officials. One of Mr. Brooks' students, Benny created the title: *Listen: An Anthology of Student Voices.*

In the scrapbook, students explored the chosen community problems through journal entries based on personal experience and original research. In one entry, Alonzo wrote,

My name is Alonzo and I attend Surrey High School in Surrey. I'm in 11th grade. My hobbies are playing football, basketball, and video games. I like to write poetry and talk to my friends. After high school I want to go to the United States Marine Corps. And after that, I would like to become a Surrey police officer.

My first entry is about the needles that you see in the streets all over Surrey. I don't see why the state won't clean it up. Children could be walking to and from school and see it. They might pick it up and hurt themselves or catch a virus or disease. If I were mayor of Surrey, I would get people who are determined to clean the city and make a difference.

In Surrey, I wonder why the police never arrest the drug dealers on the corner. The police always just drive by and never do anything . . . If I were the police, I would stop at every corner in Surrey and arrest the drug dealers . . .

Everyday after school I walk home. On the streets that I live on, there is a house where I think they do sell drugs. People have parties there. And I also think there is prostitution going on. There are fights inside and outside of the house all night long. There should be a police rundown on the house and arrest all the criminals.

As Alonzo's scrapbook entry reflects, Mr. Brooks' students faced the daily disjunctures of living in a community in which those tasked with protecting their safety, police, were seen by the students as not doing their jobs. This complicated students' civic identity development and the teacher's task, as he and they sought to find a way to see themselves as positive members of a civic body that the young people felt had not protected their interests.

In interviews, however, Mr. Brooks' students raved about the opportunity to work on a product like *Listen*. "We've never done anything like this before in school. We've never written this much. I've gone through two whole notebooks this year!" More impressive than the quantity of writing that went into developing the scrapbook was the quality and authenticity of the writing. As Mr. Brooks wrote in the scrapbook's foreword:

> What my students have presented here in *Listen*, are their own perspectives, opinions, and experiences concerning the drug trade and murders here in the city we call home. To their credit, my students in *Listen* explore and share deeply personal stories and experiences; some they still feel very uncomfortable sharing verbally. Communication through ink however, as most people could agree, is intimate and safe; a place emotionally and/or physically, many of my students [and others like them] may have not been since childhood, if ever.

Producing the scrapbook was, for the students, a meaningful engagement with the complex civic issues in which they were enmeshed, a tangible expression of their painful experiences and of their desire for change. As Mr. Brooks wrote,

But what *Listen* hopes to communicate with all of its slang, profanity, and disturbing content, is that my poorer, minority students *too* have voices, thoughts, and dreams. They are not all the same. They are not stereotypes. They do desire to see positive changes in their city, their country, their world.

Dilemmas of Civic Action Research in the Classroom

As these three cases display, enacting civic action research is a worthwhile endeavor, but not simple. Moving from emancipatory theory to practice is complex, as is attempting to integrate pedagogies based on authentic inquiry into the more constrained and artificial setting of the classroom. The dilemmas that emerged in the study schools were reflected in projects featured in research articles as well. Examining these interrelated dilemmas will help us to better structure civic action research projects for social studies classrooms.

Congruence/Disjuncture

The trajectories of these three projects demonstrate, perhaps more clearly than anything previous in this book, how students' civic experiences are deeply embedded in particular schools and communities and how the contextual nature of students' civic lives has consequences for learning and instruction. In Allwood, students' more sheltered life experiences led them to select a school-based civic problem that was more simply addressed. The new principal's rectification of the problematic backpack rule reinforced students' sense of *congruence*, the sense that those charged with their well-being had their best interests at heart and that the system was responsive to their needs. In Surrey, students' choice of a civic problem was also rooted in their daily community experiences of violence and crime. Exploring these complex problems involved a direct delving into the striking *disjuncture* between the civic ideals of security and justice and students' experiences in school and community.

Choosing to explore such problems has educational consequences that teachers will need to consider. For students at Surrey, the project was a chance for them to make a connection between learning and an issue that permeated their daily lives, a rare and meaningful occurrence. A less deeply felt problem might not have captured Mr. Brooks' students' attention in the way that the scrapbook project did. However students need extra support and a way to grapple both emotionally and analytically with such difficult problems. For Allwood students, their life experiences led them to a problem of less complexity and significance. Teachers in similar situations might consider embedding problem selection in a community study that could help students to uncover issues with broader ramifications in their own communities.

This leads to the issue of problem scope, which I will discuss next.

Problem Scope

Deep complex problems get at the heart of students' experiences of injustice, but such problems are difficult to investigate, too large to solve, and can be troubling or discouraging to engage with. Sometimes students are even part of the problem, making the research process more complex and difficult for the teacher to manage. On the other hand, narrowly bound, simple problems are easier to define and possible to address directly and accomplish some degree of change, but may be less significant and not speak to the disjunctures that many students experience.

Teachers will need to consider how much they want to help shape the scope of the problems that their students select to study. In the three study schools, teachers made different decisions, choosing small, resolvable problems in Allwood, large intractable problems in Surrey, and a variety of problems, some with the potential for student impact, in Oak Knoll. These choices impact the authenticity of the project, as will be discussed below.

Preserving Authenticity in School Settings

In school settings, teachers need to be able to hold their students accountable for learning goals. They must create assessments, judge student work, ascertain whether key skills are learned, and provide feedback, grades, and credit. The dilemma is that these mechanisms have a tendency to "schoolify" projects that are at their best when they are vital and authentic. When a project becomes "schoolified," it becomes just another school assignment, losing vigor, relevance, and interest as students try to check off what they need to do to complete the assignment with minimal effort. In this study, the Oak Knoll civic action research projects became "schoolified," with students focusing on assignment requirements, particularly in relation to the final product. Mr. Banks, uncomfortable with the research process and concerned about keeping students on track, structured the project to resemble a school project. While certainly understandable, by framing the project as another school assignment it became more difficult for Mr. Banks' students to feel ownership and investment.

Preserving the authenticity of inquiry is a major challenge to the integration of civic action research into the social studies curriculum. YPAR projects outside of the classroom can more easily be framed as authentic investigations, with students cast as activist-researchers. Such projects, however, do not need to reach the wide swathe of students served in regular public high school classrooms. The more authentic the problem, however, the more dynamic and potentially changeable it is, as will be discussed next.

The "Moving Target"

Action research is premised on the selection of a current, meaningful, relevant problem for research and action. Such projects are, by their very nature, dynamic and changing. While investigating real life problems, conditions can quickly change—the actors, context, even the problem itself. The most highly relevant problems can sometimes be "moving targets" for student research and action, changing during the process of the project.

The Allwood High School project was a clear example of a "moving target," in which the students chose a high interest, "live" problem that was in such a state of immediacy that it was resolved before the students had a chance to conduct research and form an action plan. Teachers will need to balance students' desire to tackle emergent issues with the possibility that those issues will shift and change during the course of the project, impacting their ability to produce a result. Weighing process and product, then, is another issue for such projects.

Process vs. Product

Most teachers would agree that the significant learning during these projects occurs during the process of research and investigation; this is when students gain the benefits of cooperative work with peers, analysis, and expression. The action orientation of the projects, however, causes focus to be put on the product as well. Students and teachers become invested in the problems they investigate and would like to see results. In Oak Knoll, Mr. Banks felt the end result was an important testimony of the project's success and was frustrated by what he felt were the poor efforts of his students. The scrapbook produced by Mr. Brooks' students was both process and product, satisfying for the students and their teacher despite the lack of change in Surrey's high crime rate. In Allwood, the resolution of the students' problem circumvented both process and product.

Creating a rich, collaborative, engaging process is an essential component of civic action research, as the final results of these projects are subject to factors beyond the participants' control. Teachers cannot control the outcome of students' action plans, but they can establish and support a process that can lead to meaningful civic learning and development of key civic skills. Clear and careful theoretical framing of these projects can bolster their impact.

Theoretical Framing

Projects can be framed in a range of theoretical approaches, from a critical theory approach that focuses on issues of racial and socioeconomic injustice and power imbalances, as do many YPAR projects, to a neoliberal approach that sets policy making and problem solving amid a narrative of progress and ever-increasing rights, as does Project Citizen. These frameworks can resonate differently with different groups of students and may be more or less relevant to particular problems.

In Allwood, for example, it is possible that a more critical framework might have encouraged students to select broader, more significant problems for study that connected more deeply to the rest of the curriculum. Surrey students could have used a critical lens to help them better analyze the social and historical roots of the dire problems of drugs and murder in their community. In Oak Knoll, Mr. Banks' lack of commitment to and comfort with the theoretical underpinnings of civic action research undermined his trust in the learning potential of the project.

While frequently messy and by no means perfect, the civic action research projects in Allwood, Surrey, and Oak Knoll lent a hands-on, real-life feel to students' civic learning experiences during the project year. There is much that could be done to improve the implementation of such projects into the fabric of the U.S. History curriculum. Their dynamic, imperfect messiness, however, reflects the dynamic and imperfect messiness of civic life in a democracy.

REFERENCES

Abu El-Haj, T. R. (2009a). Becoming citizens in an era of globalization and transnational migration: Re-imagining citizenship as critical practice. *Theory into Practice, 48*(4), 274–282.

Abu El-Haj, T. R. (2009b). Imagining postnationalism: Arts, citizenship education, and Arab American youth. *Anthropology and Education Quarterly, 40*(1), 1–19.

Adler, S. (1991). The education of social studies teachers. In J. Shaver (Ed.), *Handbook of research on social studies teaching and learning.* New York: Macmillan.

Andolina, M. W., Jenkins, K., Zuka, C., & Keeter, S. (2003). Habits from home, lessons from school: Influences on youth civic engagement. *PS: Political Science and Politics, 36*(2), 275–280.

Arizona Daily Star. (2010, May 12). TUSD students protest visit by Tom Horne. Video. Retrieved from http://azstarnet.com/news/local/article_5f222a2e-5df6-11df-a8d8-001cc4c03286.html?mode=video.

Atherton, H. (2000). We the people . . . Project Citizen. In S. Mann & J. Patrick (Eds.), *Education for civic engagement in democracy* (pp. 93–102). Bloomington, IN: ERIC Clearinghouse for Social Studies/Social Science Education.

Bader, L., & Pearce, D. (1983). Writing across the curriculum 7–12. *English Education, 15*(2), 105.

Battisoni, R. (1997). Service learning and democratic citizenship. *Theory Into Practice, 36*(3), 150–156.

Berg, M. J. (2004). Education and advocacy: Improving teaching and learning through student participatory action research. *Practicing Anthropology, 26*(2), 20–24.

Beyer, B. (1982). Using writing to learn social studies. *Social Studies, 73*(3), 100–105.

Bingham, A., & Christie, P. (2004). Youth action research in violence prevention: The youth survey project. *Practicing Anthropology, 26*(2), 35–39.

Bloom, L., & Ochoa, A. (1996). Responding to gender equity in the social studies curriculum. In B. G. Massialas & R. F. Allen (Eds.), *Crucial issues in teaching social studies: K-12.* New York: Wadsworth Publishing.

Butts, R. F. (1988). *The morality of democratic citizenship: Goals for civic education in the republic's third century*. Center for Civic Education, Calabasas, CA. Retrieved from http://www.civiced.org/papers/morality/morality_toc.html.

Cahill, C. (2007). Doing research with young people: Participatory research and the rituals of collective work. *Children's Geographies, 5*(3), 297–312.

Cammarota, J., & Romero, A. F. (2009). A social justice epistemology and pedagogy for Latina/o students: Transforming public education with participatory action research. *New Directions for Youth Development, 123*, 53–65.

Carnegie Corporation and CIRCLE. (2003). *The civic mission of schools report*. New York: Carnegie Corporation and CIRCLE.

Caron, E. (2004). The impact of a methods course on teaching practices: Implementing issues-centered teaching in the social studies classroom. *Journal of Social Studies Research, 28*(2), 4–19.

Center for Civic Education. (2009). *Project Citizen overview*. Calabasas, CA: Center for Civic Education. Retrieved from http://new.civiced.org/programs/project-citizen.

Center for Information and Research on Civic Learning and Engagement (CIRCLE). (2006). *Civic and political health of the nation report*. New York: CIRCLE.

Cervone, B. (1983). Students' attitudes toward studying history. *The Clearing House, 57*, 163–166.

Chapman, C. (1997). *Student interest in national news and its relation to school courses* (pp. 1–9). National Center for Education Statistics. Retrieved from http://nces.ed.gov/pubs 97/97970.pdf.

Cheney, L. (1994, Oct. 20). The end of history. *The Wall Street Journal*.

Chilcoat, G. W., & Ligon, J. A. (2001). Discussion as a means for transformative change: Social studies lessons from the Mississippi Freedom Schools. *The Social Studies*, September/October, 213–219.

Cobb, P., Confrey, J., diSessa, A., Lehrer, R., & Schauble, L. (2003). Design experiments in educational research. *Educational Researcher, 32*(1), 9–13.

Common Core State Standards Initiative. (n.d.). Retrieved from http://www.core standards.org/the-standards/english-language-arts-standards.

Connor, M. (1997). Teaching United States History thematically. *Social Education, 61*(4), 203–204.

Cook, A., & Tashlik, P. (2004). *Talk, talk, talk: Discussion-based classrooms*. New York: Teachers College Press.

Cooper, E. (2005). What do we know about out-of-school youths? How participatory action research can work for young refugees in camps. *Compare, 35*(4), 463–477.

Davis, O. L. (2005). Where is the Iraq War in the curriculum this year? Or is it missing? *Journal of Curriculum and Supervision, 20*(3), 183–187.

Degler, C. (1987). In pursuit of an American history. *American Historical Review, 12*.

Dewey, J. (1938). *Experience and education*. New York: Macmillan.

Dillon, J. T. (1994). *Using discussion in classrooms*. Bristol, PA: Open University Press.

Education World. (2010). Twenty-five great ideas for teaching current events. Retrieved from http://www.educationworld.com/a_lesson/lesson/lesson072.shtml.

Elbow, P. (1973). *Writing without teachers*. London: Oxford.

Engle, S. (1996). Foreword. In R. Evans & D.W. Saxe (Eds.), *Handbook on teaching social issues* (pp. v–viii). Washington, DC: National Council for the Social Studies.

Evans, R., & Saxe, D. W. (Eds.). (1996). *Handbook on teaching social issues*. Washington, DC: National Council for the Social Studies.

Feldman, S. (2004). The real world. *Teaching PreK-8, 6*.

Fine, M., Torre, M., Burns, A., & Payne, Y. (2007). Youth research/participatory methods for reform. In D. Thiessen & A. Cook-Sather (Eds.), *International handbook of student experience in elementary and secondary schools*. Dordrecht, The Netherlands: Kluwer Academic Publishers.

Flinders, D. J. (2006). We can and should teach the war in Iraq. *Education Digest, 71*(5), 8–12.

Freire, P. (1970). *The pedagogy of the oppressed*. New York: Continuum.

Garrison, J. (2006, August 26). Retaliation alleged for teaching on Iraq war. *The Los Angeles Times*. Retrieved from http://articles.latimes.com/2006/aug/26/local/me-recruit26.

Gitlin, T. (1996). *Twilight of common dreams*. New York: Henry Holt & Company, Inc.

Goggin, W. (1985). Writing to learn: A message for history and social studies teachers. *The Social Studies, 76*(4), 170–173.

Goodlad, J. (1983). Study of schoolings: Some findings and hypotheses. *Phi Delta Kappan, 64*(7), 465–470.

Greeno, J., & MMAP (1998). The situativity of knowing, learning and research. *American Psychologist, 53*(1), 5–26.

Grinberg, E. (2010, May 22). Texas OKs school guidelines after ideological debate. *CNN*. Retrieved from http://www.cnn.com/2010/US/05/21/texas.textbook.vote.

Gross, R. E. (1952). What's wrong with American history? *Social Education, 16*, 157–161.

Haas, M., & Laughlin, M. (2000). *Teaching current events: Its status in social studies today*. Paper presented at the annual conference of the American Educational Research Association, New Orleans.

Hahn, C. L. (1996). Research on issues-centered social studies. In R. W. Evans & D. Warren Saxe (Eds.), *Handbook on teaching social issues* (pp. 25–41). Washington, DC: National Council for the Social Studies.

Hess, D. E. (2004). Discussion in social studies: Is it worth the trouble? *Social Education*, March, 152.

Hess, D. (2009). *Controversy in the classroom: The democratic power of discussion*. New York: Routledge.

Hess, D., & Posselt, J. (2002). How students experience and learn from the discussion of controversial public issues. *Journal of Curriculum and Supervision, 17*(4), 283–314.

Kahne, J., & Middaugh, E. (2008). *Democracy for some: The civic opportunity gap in high school*. Center for Information and Research on Civic Learning and Engagement. Retrieved from http://www.civicyouth.org.

Kahne, J., & Sporte, S. (2008). Developing citizens: The impact of civic learning opportunities on students' commitment to civic participation. *American Educational Research Journal, 45*, 738–776.

Kahne, J., & Westheimer, J. (2003). Teaching democracy: What schools need to do. *Phi Delta Kappan, 85*(1), 34–66.

Kaplan, J. (2002). John Dewey at the beach. *Kappa Delta Pi Record, 38*(4), 156–159.

Kelly, A. (2003). Research as design. *Educational Researcher, 32*(1), 3–4.

Knight Abowitz, K., & Harnish, J. (2006). Contemporary discourses of citizenship. *Review of Educational Research, 76*(4), 653–690.

Larson, B. E. (1999). Influences on social studies teachers' use of classroom discussion. *The Social Studies, 73*(3), 125–132.

Larson, B. E., & Parker, W. C. (1996). What is classroom discussion? A look at teachers' conceptions. *Journal of Curriculum and Supervision, 11*(2), 110–126.

Lattimer, H. (2008). Challenging history: Essential questions in the social studies classroom. *Social Education, 72*(6), 326–329.

Lave, J. (1993). Situating learning in communities of practice. In L. Resnick, J. Levine, & S. Teasley (Eds.), *Perspectives on socially shared cognition* (pp. 63–85). Washington, DC: American Psychological Association.

Lave, J., & Wenger, E. (1991). *Situated learning: Legitimate peripheral participation.* New York: Cambridge University Press.

Levinson, M. (2007). The civic achievement gap. *CIRCLE Working Paper 51.*

Libresco, A. (2002). Current events matters for elementary school students and teachers. *Social Science Docket,* Summer–Fall, 69–70.

Lintner, T. (2006). Hurricanes and tsunamis: Teaching about natural disasters and civic responsibility in elementary classrooms. *The Social Studies,* May/June, 101–104.

Maglajlic, R. A., & Right to Know Participatory Action Research United Nations Children's Fund Bosnia and Herzegovina Team. (2004). *Child Care in Practice, 10*(2), 127–139.

McIntyre, A. (2000). Constructing meaning about violence, school, and community: Participatory action research with urban youth. *The Urban Review, 32*(2), 123–154.

McKinley Jr., J. C. (2010, March 12). Texas conservatives win curriculum change. *New York Times.* Retrieved from http://www.nytimes.com/2010/03/13/education/13texas.html?n=Top%2fReference%2fTimes%20Topics%2fOrganizations%2fB%2fBoard%20of%20Education.

Mitsakos, C., & Ackerman, A. (2009). Teaching social studies as a subversive activity. *Social Education, 73*(1), 40–42.

Morrell, E. (2004). *Becoming critical researchers: Literacy and empowerment for urban youth.* New York: Peter Lang.

National Alliance for Civic Education. (n.d.). *The importance of civic education.* Retrieved from http://www.cived.net/tioce.html.

National Council for the Social Studies (NCSS). (2009). *National curriculum standards for social studies.* Retrieved from http://www.socialstudies.org/standards/introduction.

Nelson, M. (1994). *The social studies in secondary education: A reprint of the seminal 1916 report with annotations and commentaries.* Bloomington, Indiana: ERIC Clearinghouse for Social Studies/Social Science Education.

New York Times. (2010, May 13). Citing individualism, Arizona tries to rein in ethnic studies in school. Retrieved from http://www.nytimes.com/2010/05/14/education/14arizona.html?scp=2&sq=arizona%20%22ethnic%20studies%22&st=cse.

Nystrand, M., Gamoran, A., & Carbonaro, W. (1998). *Towards an ecology of learning: The case of classroom discourse and its effects on writing in high school English and social studies* (pp. 1–27). CELA Research Report, Series 11001. New York: National Center on English Learning and Achievement, University of Albany, SUNY.

Okolo, C., Ferretti, R., & MacArthur, C. (2007) Talking about history: Discussions in a middle school inclusive classroom. *Journal of Living Disabilities, 40*(20), 154–165.

Owens, D. C., & Jones, K. T. (2004). Adapting the youth participatory action research model to serve LBGTQ youth of color. *Practicing Anthropology, 26*(2), 25–29.

Park, P. (1993). What is participatory research? A theoretical and methodological perspective. In P. Park, M. Brydon-Miller, B. Hall, & T. Jackson (Eds.), *Voices of change: Participatory research in the United States and Canada* (pp. 1–19). Westport, CT: Bergin & Garvey.

Parker, W. C., & Hess, D. (2001). Teaching with and for discussion. *Teaching and Teacher Education, 17,* 273–289.

Passe, J., & Evans, R. (1996). Discussion methods in an issue-centered curriculum. In R. W. Evans & D. Warren Saxe (Eds.), *Handbook on teaching social issues* (pp. 81–88). Washington, DC: National Council for the Social Studies.

Pescatore, C. (2007). Current events as empowering literacy: For English and social studies teachers. *Journal of Adolescent and Adult Literacy, 51*(4), 326–339.

Peterson, M. D. (1960*). The Jefferson image in the American mind.* New York: Oxford University Press.

Powers, J. L., & Tiffany, J. S. (2006). Engaging youth in participatory research and evaluation. *Journal of Public Health Management Practice*, November supplement, S79–S87.

Root, S., & Northup, J. (2007). *Project Citizen evaluation report.* Denver, CO: RMC Research Corporation.

Rubin, B. (2007). "There's still not justice": Youth civic identity development amid distinct school and community contexts. *Teachers College Record, 109*(2), 449–481.

Rubin, B. C., & Hayes, B. (2010). "No backpacks" vs. "Drugs and murder": The promise and complexity of youth civic action research. *Harvard Educational Review, 80*(3), 149–175.

Rubin, B. C., Hayes, B., & Benson, K. (2009). "It's the worst place to live": Urban youth and the challenge of school-based civic learning. *Theory into Practice, 48*(3), 213–221.

Rubin, B. C., & Jones, M. (2007). Student action research: Reaping the benefits for students and school leaders. *National Association of Secondary School Principals Bulletin, 91*(4), 363–378.

Sabo, K. (2003). Editor's notes. *New Directions for Evaluation, 98*, 1–11.

Schensul, S. L., LoBianco, L., & Lombardo, C. (2004). Youth participatory action research (Youth PAR) in public schools: Opportunities and challenges in an inner-city high school. *Practicing Anthropology, 26*(2), 10–14.

Schultz, B. (2008) *Spectacular things happen along the way.* New York: TC Press.

Sharp, K. (2009). *A survey of Appalachian middle and high school teacher perceptions of controversial current events instruction.* Paper presented at the annual meeting of The National Council for the Social Studies, Atlanta, GA.

Singleton, L. R., & Giese, J. R. (1996). Preparing citizens to participate in democratic discourse: The public issues model. In R.W. Evans & D. Warren Saxe (Eds.), *Handbook on teaching social issues* (pp. 59–65). Washington, DC: National Council for the Social Studies.

Soule, S. (2006). *A campaign to promote civic education: A model of how to get education for democracy back into U.S. classrooms in all fifty states.* Paper presented at the International Conference on School Reform: Research and Practice, Vancouver, December 13–14.

Stotsky, S. (1990). Connecting reading and writing to civic education. *Educational Leadership, 47*, 72–73.

Stoudt, B. (2009). The role of language & discourse in the investigation of privilege: Using Participatory Action Research to discuss theory, develop methodology, and interrupt power. *The Urban Review, 41*(1), 7–28.

Sumrall, W., & Schillinger, D. N. (2004). A student-directed model for designing a science/social studies curriculum. *The Social Studies,* Jan/Feb, 5–10.

Sydlo, S. J., Schensul, J. J., Owens, D. C., Brase, M. K., Wiley, K. N., Berg, M. J., Baez, E., & Schensul, D. (2004). *Participatory action research curriculum for empowering youth.* Hartford, CT: The Institute for Community Research.

Torney-Purta, J., & Wilkenfeld, B. (2009). *Paths to 21st century competencies through civic education.* Chicago, IL: American Bar Association Division for Public Education.

Torre, M. (2009). Participatory action research and critical race theory: Fueling spaces for nos-otras to research. *The Urban Review, 41*(1), 106–120.

Tredway, L. (1995). Socratic seminars: Engaging students in intellectual discourse. *Educational Leadership*, September, 26–29.

Tuck, E. (2009). Re-visioning action: Participatory action research and indigenous theories of change. *The Urban Review, 41*(1), 47–65.

Turner, T. (1995). Riding the rapids of current events! *Social Studies, 86*(3), 117.

Wadsworth, Y. (1998). What is participatory action research? *Action Research International*, Paper 2. Retrieved from http://www.scu.edu.au/schools/gcm/ar/ari/p-ywadsworth98.html.

Watts, R., Griffith, D., & Abdul-Adil, J. (1999). Sociopolitical development as an antidote for oppression—theory and action. *American Journal of Community Psychology, 27*(2), 255–271.

Weiss, I. R. (1978). *Report of the 1977 National Survey of Science, Mathematics, and Social Studies Education.* Research Triangle Park, NC: Center for Educational Research and Evaluation.

White, R. (1995). How thematic teaching can transform history instruction. *The Clearing House, 63*(3), 160–162.

Whitehouse, J. A. (2008). Discussion with a difference: Questions and cooperative learning. *Ethos, 16*(1), 11–15.

Wiggins, G., & McTighe, J. (1998). *Understanding by design.* Upper Saddle River, NJ: Prentice-Hall, Inc.

Wilen, W. W. (2003). Conducting effective issue based discussions in social studies classrooms. *International Journal of Social Education, 18*(1), 99–110.

Wolk, S. (2003). Teaching for critical literacy in social studies. *Social Studies. 94*(3), 101–106.

Yilmaz, K. (2007). Historical empathy and its implications for classroom practices in schools. *History Teacher, 40*(3), 331–337.

Zukin, C., Keeter, S., Andolina, M., Jenkins, K., & Delli Carpini, M. (2006). *A new engagement? Political participation, civic life, and the changing American citizen.* New York: Oxford University Press.

ABOUT THE AUTHOR

Beth C. Rubin is Associate Professor in the Department of Educational Theory, Policy, and Administration at Rutgers University where she is co-coordinator of the social studies education program. In her research she uses a sociocultural approach to consider issues of equity in U.S. public schools, examining student learning and identity development at the intersection of classroom life and structural inequality. Among her publications are *Civic Education for Diverse Citizens in Global Times: Rethinking Theory and Practice and Critical Voices in School Reform: Students Living Through Change*.

INDEX

active learning 23, 123; *see also* progressive education
adult life, preparing for 70, 100
Afghanistan 32, 55–56
African American students 5, 15
AIDS advocacy 94
Allwood 11; *see also* Allwood High School
Allwood High School: civic action research in 125–127, 136, 138, 139; preparation for life after school 13–14; state proficiency tests 14–15; students' attendance data 13; students' demographics 11, 12–13, 16; students' disciplinary data 13; teacher's characteristic 16–17; *see also* Allwood
Andolina, M. W. 46
attendance data 13
aware students 6

Beyer, B. 71
Bill of Rights 5, 89–90
Black Muslims 83–85; *see also* Black people
Black people 38; *see also* Black Muslims
Bloom, L. 22
Brewer, Jan 1
Burke, Edmund 25, 53, 134
Butts, R. Freedman 104

candidates' forum 80–82, 110–113
capitalism 31
Center for Civic Education 121

Center for Information and Research on Civic Learning and Engagement (CIRCLE) 99
Cervone, B. 21
Cheney, Lynne 2n.2
child labor 34, 54
Chinese Exclusion Act 109
Chinese for Affirmative Action 2
chronological approach 3, 25, 33, 37–39; and current events teaching 103–104, 115–116
CIRCLE, *see* Center for Information and Research on Civic Learning and Engagement
citizen groups 2
citizenship 5, 109; skills 121–122
civic action 5, 23; *see also* civic action research
civic action research 20, 117–139; congruence/disjuncture 36; dilemmas of 136–139; in Allwood High School 125–127, 136, 138, 139; in Oak Knoll High School 128–131, 137, 138, 139; in Surrey High School 132–136, 138, 139; preserving authenticity of inquiry 137; problems as "moving targets" 138; problem scope issue 137; process vs. product 138; project approach 123–136; Project Citizen approach 121–123; theoretical framing 138–139; youth participatory action research (YPAR) approach 118–123

civic affairs 98
civic engagement 99
civic identity 5–9, 25
civic literacy 27
Civic Mission of Schools, The 45, 97, 98, 104
civic participation 68–69
civic problems 5, 7–8, 20, 24, 80, 118, 122; *see also* civic action research
civic skill building strands 10–11; *see also* civic action research; current events; discussion; expressive activities; writing
civil conversation 19
civil rights 32, 37, 91
Civil Rights News Broadcast project 71, 82–85
College and Career Readiness Standards for Literacy in History/Social Studies 70, 85
Committee on Social Studies 24
Common Core State Standards for English Language Arts & Literacy in History/Social Studies 70
communication 68–69; *see also* expressive activities; writing
Communism 31
Communities United Against Racism in Education (CURE) 2
complacent students 6
Conflict and Resolution theme 25, 27–28, 32–35, 38, 43, 54, 78–79, 113
congruence 5, 6, 136
Connor, M. 29, 32, 33
conversation 41
Cook, A. 42
creative expressions 80–85
critical capacities 69–70, 99
critical theory 120, 138
CURE, *see* Communities United Against Racism in Education
current events 19, 97–116; and chronological approach 103–104, 115–116; and thematic approach 115; as controversial 103; best teaching practices 104–105; connecting to history 107; difficulties teaching 102–105; electoral politics 110–112; political issues 110–112; project approach 105–116; reasons for learning 98–102; role of essential questions 106, 109, 115; separation from curriculum 102; students' own perspectives 112–115; trivializing approach 102–103

DBR, *see* design-based research
debates 19, 85–87
Declaration of Independence 89–90
Democratic Party 27, 101, 110, 112
demographics 11–13, 16
design-based research (DBR) 9–10
Dewey, John 121, 123
Dillon, J. T. 42, 51
disability rights 92
disciplinary data 13
discouraged students 6–7
discussion 19, 41–65; civic benefits 45–49; creating safe setting 59–60; definitions 42; forms of 52–59; "good" 41–42, 61; key principles for teaching with 59–65; lack of in schools 49–50; structure of 60; teachers' concerns about 50–51; teacher's role in 61–65; topics 61; training students to participate in 60–61; use of questions in 61; *see also* Socratic seminar; structured conversation; Take-a-Stand
disjuncture 5, 6, 136
do-now questions 73–78
drugs 53, 85–86, 132–135

Economics theme 27–28, 32, 54, 79, 88
Education World 102
Elbow, Peter 69
electoral politics 80–82, 110–112
empires 24
empowered students 7
empowerment 120
essays 19, 87, 88; essential questions as prompts 91–92
essential questions 19, 21–40; and chronological approach 37–39; and current events teaching 106, 109, 115; and expressive activities 91–94; and social science journals 74, 79; and students' social movement presentations 92–94; and thematic approach 27–33, 37; and writing 69, 91–94; as essay prompts 91–92; benefits for learning 23–26; definitions 23; recommendations for using 40
ethnic studies 1
Evans, R. 24
expressive activities 67–95; and communication skills 68–69; and critical capacities 69–70; and essential questions 91–94; and historical

empathy 71–72; benefits for learning
68–72; creative expressions 80–85;
debates 85–87; *see also* writing

Feldman, Sandra 100, 105
Freire, Paulo 119

gay rights movement 92
genocide 34
Gitlin, Todd 2
Goggin, W. 69
Government theme 27–28
graduation rates 13–14

Haas, M. 103
Handbook on Teaching Social Issues 24
healthcare 111
"heavy information" 31
Hess, D. 52
Horne, Tom 1

ICR, *see* Institute for Community
Research
immigration 37–38, 106, 108–109,
112–113
Institute for Community Research (ICR)
120
Internet 102
Iraq war 57–58, 103, 107, 111, 113–114
Irish potato famine 108
issues-centred curricula 24; *see also*
thematic approach; themes

Japanese Internment 89–90
Jefferson, Thomas 69
journal prompts 19
journals, *see* social studies journals

Kahne, J. 7
Kaplan, J. 123
knowledge: approaches to 22–25, 36, 50;
civic 5, 101–102, 121; research to build
71
K–W–L chart 92

Larson, B. E. 45
Latino rights movement 92
Latino students 5, 15
Lattimer, H. 23
Laughlin, M. 103
learning 3–4, 10, 24
letters 87–90
Libresco, A. 105

Lintner, T. 101
listening skills 45, 46, 99

Malcolm X 83–85
Man and His Changing Society 2n.2
McLeroy, Don 1n.1
McTighe, J. 23, 27
Meet the Candidates, *see* candidates'
forum
Middaugh, E. 7
migration 37–38
mock news conferences 19
Movement of People theme 27–28,
37–38, 108

National Association for the Advancement
of Colored People 2
National Center for Education Statistics
99
National Chicano Moratorium
Committee 2
National Coalition of Education
Activists 2
National Council for the Social Studies 23,
24, 97–98
National History Standards 2n.2
National Household Educational Survey
99
neoliberal approach 139
newscast 82–85
news conferences, mock 19
news media, and civic engagement 99
NGOs, *see* nongovernmental
organizations
No Child Left Behind Act 15
nongovernmental organizations (NGOs)
119

Oak Knoll 12; *see also* Oak Knoll High
School
Oak Knoll High School: civic action
research in 128–131, 137–139;
preparation for life after school 13–14;
state proficiency tests 14–15; students'
attendance data 13; students'
demographics 12–13, 16; students'
disciplinary data 13; teacher's
characteristic 17–18; *see also* Oak Knoll
Ochoa, A. 22
open questions 24, 35–36, 115;
see also essential questions
oral expression 19, 46, 99;
see also expressive activities

Parker, W. C. 45, 52
Participatory Action Research Curriculum for Empowering Youth 120
persuasive abilities 69
persuasive letters 87–90
persuasive speeches 19, 87–88
persuasive writing 72–73, 85, 87–91
Pescatore, C. 99
Pledge of Allegiance 4–5
political apathy 112
political issues 110–112
political parties 27, 101, 110, 112
presentations 19, 92–94
"problem-posing" approach 8
pro-choice movement 92
progressive education 24, 119, 123
Project Citizen 119, 121–123, 138
pro-life movement 92–93
public affairs 97; *see also* current events

questions: do-now 73–78; open 24, 35–36, 115; role in discussion 61; *see also* essential questions

racial equality 85
racial profiling 130
racism 85, 130
Republican Party 1, 27, 101, 110, 112
roundtable 82
Rugg, Harold 2n.2

Schultz, Brian 117, 122
September 11 attacks 48
Social Change theme 23, 27–30, 32
social inequality 120
social movement presentations 92–94
social studies journals 72–74, 76–80
Socratic seminar 19, 25, 34, 48–49, 63; characteristics 52–54; training students to participate in 60
speeches 87
state proficiency tests 14–15
Stotsky, S. 68–69
structured conversation 57–59
students: access to civic education best practices 7, 98; African American 5, 15; aware 6; complacent 6; discouraged 6–7; empowered 7; experiences of social studies teaching 3, 21–22, 25; inequities in civic knowledge distribution 101; Latino 5, 15; of Allwood High School 11–16; of Oak Knoll High School 12–16; of Surrey

High School 11–16; perspectives on citizenship 5; perspectives on current issues 112–115; teaching relevant to personal experience of 34, 48–49, 53–54, 77–78, 100–101
Surrey 12; *see also* Surrey High School
Surrey High School: civic action research in 132–136, 138, 139; preparation for life after school 13–14; state proficiency tests 14–15; students' attendance data 13; students' demographics 11, 12–13, 16; students' disciplinary data 13; teacher's characteristic 18; *see also* Surrey

Take-a-Stand 19, 34–36, 43–44, 109, 113–114; as "discussion in motion" 54–57
talkshow 82
Tashlik, P. 42
terrorism 56–57
Texas State Board of Education 1
thematic approach 19, 23–26, 29–33, 37–40; and current events teaching 106, 115; *see also* themes
themes 27–29; Conflict and Resolution 25, 27–28, 32–35, 38, 43, 54, 78–79, 113; Economics 27–28, 32, 54, 79, 88; Government 27–28; Movement of People 27–28, 37–38, 108; recommendations for using 40; Social Change 23, 27–30, 32
thinking skills 46, 99; *see also* critical capacities
Torney-Purta, J. 100
Tredway, L. 52
Turner, T. 102

"understanding by design" approach 27
UNICEF 119

Vietnam war 57–58, 107–108
violence 25, 119, 120

Wadsworth, Y. 119
war: Afghanistan 32, 55–56; Iraq 57–58, 103, 107, 111, 113–114; just 33, 79, 91; Vietnam 57–58, 107–108
war economy 32, 57–59
White, Brian 94
White, R. 34
Wiggins, G. 23, 27
Wilen, W. W. 50

Wilkenfeld, B. 100
Wolk, S. 42, 49, 69
writing 67–95; and communication skills
    68–69; and critical capacities 69–70;
    and essential questions 69, 91–94; and
    historical empathy 71–72; benefits for
    learning 68–72; college and career
    readiness standards 70–71; do-now
    questions 73–78; persuasive 72–73, 85,
87–91; social studies journals 72–74,
76–80

youth participatory action research
    (YPAR) 118–123, 137, 138
YPAR, *see* youth participatory action
    research

Zukin, C. 42

Made in the USA
Middletown, DE
08 March 2015